THE MARRIAGE BED

THE MARRIAGE BED is very different from the mass of material published in recent years on sex and marriage. It is not a book about sexual skills and techniques, sexual problems, case histories ("Frank and Helen have been married for twenty years..."), nor does it have quotes from experts and authorities.

THE MARRIAGE BED is a book about strengthening a couple's sexual relationship, suggesting that if serious problems exist, the couple should seek professional help. It is a prescription for action without psychological theories or discussion. It is a prescription for marital health and emotional well-being.

THE MARRIAGE BED is based on the conviction that a lasting love deserves the lifelong care and thought that we would use to preserve, protect, and nourish whatever is precious to us—in this case, marriage.

The Marriage Bed

*RENEWING LOVE, FRIENDSHIP,
TRUST AND ROMANCE*

WILLIAM M. WOMACK, M.D.
and FRED F. STAUSS

NEW HARBINGER PUBLICATIONS, INC.

Copyright © 1991 by New Harbinger Publications, Inc.
                     5674 Shattuck Avenue
                     Oakland, CA 94609

ISBN 1-879237-27-X Paperback
ISBN 1-879237-28-8 Hardcover

First New Harbinger printing, January, 1992 5,000 copies

Originally published by Madrona Publishers, Inc., Seattle, Washington.

Library of Congress Cataloging-in-Publication Data

Womack, William M.
  The marriage bed.

  1. Sex in marriage. I. Strauss, Fred F., 1948-
II. Title.
HQ31.W787 186   646.7 8   86-18147

Preface

BOOKS, like marriages, grow and change over the course of time. This book has been growing for the last fourteen years, starting life as a research project at the University of Wisconsin Medical School, to design a self-help sex-therapy program.

It was first published as an eight-page manual which grew into a full-length book published in 1976, entitled *Sex Therapy at Home*, coauthored by David Kass, M.D., and Fred F. Stauss. Ongoing evaluation of the program continued at the University of Wisconsin Medical School at the same time further work on it was taking place at the University of Washington Medical School. The book's next-to-last form was as a self-help computer program.

During these last fourteen years, hundreds of people have been involved in bringing *The Marriage*

Bed to its present form: professionals in behavior therapy, family counseling, sex therapy, program design and evaluation, computer interviewing and computer instruction, along with numerous couples who took part in the program and volunteered their own experiences.

The program itself is based on a combination of respected and well-tested techniques developed primarily by sex researchers and counselors including Masters and Johnson, LoPiccolo, Wolpe, and Lazarus. But as experience grew, it became clear that while the basic premises were correct as far as they went, one significant element was lacking to provide the maximum benefit to the greatest number of people.

Instead of seeking help for sexual problems, most married couples concerned with the sexual aspects of their relationship simply want to add more pleasure, satisfaction and comfort to what may already be a solid commitment. Thus, *The Marriage Bed* as presented here is not a book about solving sexual problems, but a program for strengthening the bonds of marriage through promoting the growth of a couple's sexual relationship. It is not a book about illness but a book about emotional health and well-being. Its most basic premise is that enduring passion results from a combination of love, friendship, trust and romance; and that if sexual passion can endure, the likelihood of a rich, satisfying and lasting marriage is much greater.

Fred Stauss has been the coordinator of the research project since its inception. He has also been the person who has gathered everyone's ideas, put them in a usable format and done most of the writing.

William Womack, M.D., has provided the professional expertise and the information needed to change *The Marriage Bed* from just another sex book to a book that provides the basis for lasting passion. He has effectively linked the excitement of sexual passion to the love, friendship, trust and romance that create and nourish it.

William M. Womack, M.D.

Fred F. Stauss

Contents

1. You Deserve the Best   3

2. New Beginnings   8

3. Friends and Lovers   14

4. Taking Chances Together   19

5. Courting   28

6. A School for Pleasure   39

7. Step 1: Getting to Know You   61

8. Step 2: Giving and Getting   72

    Special Section for Women   85

9. Step 3: Lighting the Fire   88

10. Step 4: Show and Tell   99

11. Step 5: Learning the Territory   116

12. Step 6: Fun and Fantasy   153

13. Step 7: The Ultimate Sharing   173

14. Things to Remember   188

THE MARRIAGE BED

CHAPTER 1

You Deserve the Best

SEX is undeniably a big part of every marriage. Whether a couple talks about it or ignores it, their sex life greatly influences how they feel about themselves, each other and their marriage. A gratifying sex life not only makes marriage better, but makes all of life better. Satisfying sex leads to a greater appreciation of sex itself, one's partner and oneself. While a satisfying sexual relationship can't necessarily save a marriage, the absence of a satisfying sex life can certainly impair one.

The benefits of a satisfying married sex life are bountiful. In the first place, sex is pleasure. It's a great way to put aside the struggles of life for a while and simply feel good. When each partner feels self-confident in a sexual relationship, they each feel more confidence in their bodies and in life in general. This attitude, in turn, grows into a general increase in self-esteem. Sex also provides shared feelings—feelings that range from love, caring and closeness, to playfulness and fun. As this sharing grows, a special bond develops between the two lovers—a bond that strengthens the marriage.

While some fortunate couples find that reality even surpasses their expectations, most of us admit to ourselves that we want more from our love-making. Our dreams of unbounded love, relaxing sensuous contact and ravenous passion (which everyone else is supposed to be getting) are seldom matched by our own experience. We keep the secret that our intimacy does not match our fantasies. This is especially disappointing because, generally speaking, most of us had exciting, enjoyable sex with our partner when we first became intimate.

Realistically, however, some disappointments should not be surprising. To begin with, most of us have grown up with inhibitions about sex imposed on us by society. As if that weren't enough, throughout our lives we encounter other obstacles to sexual intimacy. Couples in their thirties, for example, often find that the pressures of building a family and one or two careers take up much of the energy that had previously been directed toward their relationship. As they reach their forties, they may face dead-ends in their careers, the empty nest of a house without children or just a sense of purposelessness—the so-called mid-life crisis. Couples in their fifties must accept their bodies' aging, which may bring a sense of loss of youthful appeal. For couples in their sixties there are the problems of adapting to retirement and the struggles for self-esteem that often follow. As they reach their seventies, they may feel that they are too old to enjoy sex (largely, of course, because society says they are). No wonder so many of us simply settle for sex lives that are *good enough*—if not what we'd like them to be—rather than putting much energy into improvement.

The key to a rich sex life is actually quite simple for most of us. Satisfying sex occurs when the partners have each learned to be comfortable with their own sexuality, their lover and the sexual situation. Instead of sexual performance being the primary focus, both partners learn to enjoy each moment of each sexual activity. As this happens, they both become more and more satisfied with the sexual relationship. Feelings grow deeper and desire occurs more frequently. Although arousal and orgasms are more likely to happen whenever and however wanted, sex becomes more and more satisfying without the *need* for them.

Sexual comfort is what this book is all about. No matter what your unfulfilled sexual desires or what problems you may be encountering, increasing your sexual comfort should result in far more rewarding sex and will allow you to gradually mold your sex life to fit your own unique desires. Then, as your sex life begins to change, you will most likely realize that this gradual growth is not just temporary, but something that will go on for the rest of your lives. Some noticeable changes will probably occur almost immediately; as time goes on, more subtle changes will take place as well. These changes are only the beginning of a life-long process as you add richness to your sex life and as you adapt to growth in yourself and your spouse.

Making oneself comfortable with sex is a learning and relearning process. The barriers that inhibit our ability to fully enjoy sex—fear, guilt and performance expectations for example—can be broken down. The more comfortable we feel, the more we enjoy sex.

Making your sex life more enjoyable is just like going to school—except that it's a lot more fun! In school you learned simple arithmetic before you learned algebra; here, you'll begin by learning (or relearning) to enjoy the early steps of sexual intimacy on your way to learning to enjoy *all* the steps. This is a sex education course with homework, a format for the two of you to use to improve your love-making by following a very specific course of study. In the process, you'll complete more and more intimate assignments while always keeping in mind the goal of remaining *comfortable*. As you learn to enjoy each of these steps, increased passion and pleasure will arrive naturally.

You may find that your courtship has started all over again. You will share many of the pleasures that you enjoyed in the beginning of your relationship; but this time you will be doing it with the benefits of having known each other for years and having shared the experiences of those years. In essence, you'll be renewing the closeness of your relationship.

As you improve your sex life, you will also improve the other parts of your marriage. Both of you will learn to express your feelings more easily and completely. This will help you understand how to please yourself and your spouse more, and in turn, will help you understand and deal more quickly and easily with any conflicts that arise between you. You'll learn more about how to share love and pleasure and have fun doing it.

This approach requires a strong commitment. What happens depends on you. Like anything else, the more effort you put into it, the more benefit you receive. This book provides the framework, but it is you who will make the changes. As you go through the assignments, you may be changing and challenging many entrenched personal and marital habits. While many changes will come easily, others may be troublesome. Your personal commitment to going through all the steps is critical.

Getting your partner involved will be one of your first assignments. You need to be comfortable not only with your own sexuality, but also with your partner's. You will each be opening your eyes to new possibilities, but neither of you needs to feel forced to try anything you don't want to do. You will simply try to have more fun together.

No matter what sex means to you, you deserve to have the best sex life possible for you and to enjoy life to the fullest. Nearly everyone has the ability and the means to fulfill their sexual desires. If you want to put more love, excitement and fun into your love-making, then decide now to get started.

CHAPTER 2

New Beginnings

COUPLES usually stay together because there is "something" that each person gets from the relationship. It may be the comfort and pleasure of companionship. It may be social or financial security or the desire to raise children together. It can also be that elusive feeling called love. The list of possible reasons for desiring to remain a couple is almost endless. Although in each case the specific reason or reasons are sometimes hard to see, all that really matters for a happy relationship is that each person likes being with the other.

Sexual excitement is one of the more common reasons for individuals choosing to become a couple. The power of sexual passion to awaken each partner's enjoyment of life can provide couples with enough reason to get together and stay together until friendship, trust and commitment have had time to build the solid foundation of a long-term relationship. Although the initial high energy of passion may fade with time, sex can remain an important part of that special something that bonds the couple together.

Sex has such bonding power because it is the most intimate way for two people to know one another. Lovers express their love by giving their partners the extraordinary physical and emotional pleasure that only sex can provide. Sex is especially important in many marriages because a lot of people receive much of their caring from others through touching, and many people, especially men, only infrequently touch other people, except during sex, in an openly caring manner like hugging or kissing.

We get an enormous amount of self-worth from a satisfying sex life, which gives us the feeling of being valued, important and special. During sex, we can easily and immediately see that our lover believes that we are truly important. Our self-esteem grows with the sense of power that we feel when we give so much pleasure to another person and experience the delight of seeing our lover feel that pleasure. Our self-esteem also grows from having a partner who gives us pleasure. A satisfying sex life leads to a spiral of continually escalating self-esteem for each lover.

Every part of our lives benefits from the nourishing and nurturing we get from a satisfying sex life. As with satisfying jobs, friends and hobbies, the nourishment we receive from sex leads to an increased sense of creativity and the confidence that we can fulfill more of our own desires. It also leads to a greater enjoyment of life by providing us with more enthusiasm to pursue our desires and by helping us achieve a positive acceptance of life as it is.

Besides making life feel good, nourishing sex gives us an emotional cushion that makes the bad times seem not so bad. When things are not going as well as we would like, we may question our worth or the direction of our lives. The intimacy of sex helps us continue to feel important and not so burdened by our struggles.

On the other hand, when a marital relationship begins to falter, sexual pleasure is often the first area of the relationship to suffer. A breakdown may occur in desire, physical ability or emotional pleasure. A breakdown in sexual pleasure often leads to an increased emotional separation of the couple in every aspect of the relationship. Each partner becomes more cautious and less open about sharing feelings. Although it may be just the opposite of what each partner wants, each tends to gradually eliminate the other a little more from their life.

The caring and touching of sex make us feel valued, and if they disappear, we lose that feeling of being special. When this happens, we begin to look for ways to compensate for that loss. We may put more effort into our job or our children to get back that feeling of being important. It's not unusual at this time for people to turn to affairs to recover some of that feeling. Almost always, however, no matter what alternative we choose, a noticeable decrease in the liveliness of the marriage occurs.

Trouble in a marriage, particularly in the sexual relationship, often shows up when the partners assume that each knows all they need to know about the other and can even predict the other's behavior. As a result, the feeling grows that the marriage is simply routine and ultimately boring. This attitude limits each partner's desire to learn more about and from each other. As the boredom grows, the partners begin to take each other even more for granted. The value of each one's uniqueness and specialness is brought into question, and the value of the relationship is in deep question.

A marriage becomes still more painful when the partners not only believe that they can predict each other's behavior, but expect that the behavior will be undesirable. The joys of a once rewarding relationship are replaced by repeated disappointment. At this stage, the marital bond quickly deteriorates. Since each partner thinks they know what to expect of their spouse, they tend to react without thinking, and the bond continues to weaken.

As they both lose the feeling of being wanted or important, they feel extremely vulnerable and less willing to take risks. Each is more likely to close off potentially threatening intimate discussions. Instead of the intimacy and openness that were a part of the blossoming relationship, both are now more likely to grow more protective of their own needs and ignore the needs of the other. Little by little, that something that each partner really liked about the other loses importance, and concern about one's own importance comes first.

There are ways to strengthen both the non-sexual and sexual bonds, but they take time, effort and some risk. Each partner must learn to stop responding to the other automatically and start responding in a thoughtful and positive manner. Each must make a commitment to rebuild the bond. Each must be willing to accept responsibility for his or her own pleasure and be willing to cooperate with the other in fulfilling the desires of both. Each must be willing to take a new look at their marriage and see that there is still a great deal to learn about themselves and each other.

To sum up: couples need to exert the same energy to keep their marriage alive that they would expect to put into their careers or raising their children. Too often when the marriage is taken for granted it loses intimacy, passion and commitment. The best way of renewing sexual excitement in marriage is to make each partner feel more valuable. As both begin to feel more valued and more secure, they are willing to take the risks that go with change. This courage to change leads to greater trust and intimacy and the willingness to work together to challenge old ways, habits and ideas. The result is an increased freshness in the sexual relationship and the marriage.

Although there are many ways of getting each partner to feel more valuable, one of the most effective ways is to create the excitement of starting something new together. But beginning again takes effort. Each partner must be willing to risk giving up old ways and trying new ones. Loving and caring will be called for, as will patience and trust. Both must believe that the marriage bond is precious enough to work at preserving and strengthening it. Both must be willing to bring it back to the marriage bed.

CHAPTER **3**

Friends and Lovers

LASTING passion in marriage depends on a combination of friendship, trust and romance. Sexual infatuation may have drawn a couple together initially, but it is *friendship* that keeps them together. If the partners feel that they are getting out of the relationship what they want, each tries even harder to make it that much more solid, and their marriage and their sex life stay alive and healthy.

Friendship is easier to recognize than to define. In very simple terms, friends are the people we most enjoy being with, even though we may not know or care why. Friends, you could say, are the cheerleaders of life. They accept us for what we are and encourage us to be who we want to be.

Friendship usually begins with the sharing of

common interests, and from this a bond is built. Friendship lasts, however, because of the acceptance of differences. As we accept each other as separate individuals, we feel more secure to be ourselves and the bond grows even stronger. On the other hand, friendship breaks down when we no longer trust someone to accept us as we are. Lovers need to be particularly protective of their friendship, because they generally have greater expectations of one another than "just friends" do, and these expectations can make accepting each other tougher.

As friendship grows, trust grows. We trust that we will not suffer by showing our vulnerability. We believe that our friend will protect us as we would protect ourselves. Trust leads to taking even greater risks of sharing, without being afraid that the friend will take advantage of us or cause us pain. Married couples who are friends easily share responsibilities and private thoughts. Their trust in each other allows them to be themselves without worrying about being rejected or embarrassed.

For some couples trust grows quickly, while for others it takes a long time. Similarly, the erosion of trust can happen either quickly or gradually. Over time, each of us decides how far we will trust others. When we do not feel secure, we pay extra attention to protecting ourselves as do others when they feel insecure with us. Since we can't directly change someone else's feelings, we can only hope that their trust in us will grow as we consistently show care and respect for them. It is frustrating to have to accept that being consistent in our actions is far more important in building trust than the easier way of simply asking someone to trust us.

While friendship and trust say that a person is *accepted*, romance takes friendship one step further by saying that the person is *special, unique, the best in the world*. A phone call, a card, flowers, or any little surprise can provide that special message.

Combining romance with friendship is very important to keeping a marriage alive and growing. Friendship provides the foundation for a long-term commitment and romance keeps it special. As couples learn this, the relationship will become increasingly rich.

All this takes thoughtful attention. Couples too often realize that the effort is needed only after the relationship has begun to falter. Obviously, the more one gets from the relationship, the more one is willing to put into it. And the more one puts in, the more one gets out.

The most important person to be a friend to is *yourself*. As a good friend to yourself, you should take good care of yourself and treat yourself as well as you would others—not always an easy job, since most of us are better at taking care of other people. This care means that you accept yourself for what you are, and that you let yourself be who you want to be. You need to learn to give yourself what you want, both physically and emotionally. Even if you begin to feel a little selfish, that's OK. You are simply taking care of your own needs and allowing others to take care of theirs. As you and your spouse each learn to take better care of yourselves, the two of you will find yourselves more caring of each other.

To satisfy some of your desires, you may want help from your partner. You may even feel that you need help. While wanting help is OK, problems begin when you expect that your partner *has to* help you. It gets worse when you expect your partner to know what you want and to help you without your even having to ask. Expectations like these get many couples into a lot of trouble. It's best to start with the assumption that you are two separate individuals who are each trying to be comfortable with life. So when you want your partner's help you need to ask for it. You don't need to explain *why* you want something, just that you *do.* (Explaining often implies that what you want isn't quite OK and needs justifying.) If you don't ask, you can't expect help. And even if you do ask, it doesn't mean that your partner will or should be able to help you. You should expect that your partner will not stand in your way, but you can't expect that you will automatically get the help that you asked for. However, no matter what the results, you should always assume that you have the right and the responsibility to try to satisfy your own needs.

As you learn to recognize that it's OK for you to be you, you need to give your partner the same freedom and, ideally, to encourage it. But don't be surprised if you have trouble giving your partner this freedom—chances are it'll take some practice.

Here are some useful rules for friendship in marriage. Some may call for conscious effort at first, but over time they will become second nature.

1. Accept yourself for who you are, and your partner for who he or she is.
2. Be who you want to be.
3. Remember that *your* needs and desires are as important as anyone else's.
4. Don't always feel you have to *explain* your needs and desires.
5. Be willing to ask for what you want. If you don't ask, you can't expect to receive.
6. Don't expect too much from your partner. If you ask for help, it doesn't mean that you will always get it. Your partner has a duty to not stand in your way, but not necessarily to help you.
7. Although you do not always need to help your partner, do not stand in your partner's way.

Begin rebuilding your friendship, trust and romance outside the bedroom. Keep in mind that sex and romance start long before you reach the bed and continue long after the last orgasm.

CHAPTER 4

Taking Chances Together

CREATING a richer sexual relationship requires that both you and your partner want to. Making changes by yourself to increase your own sexual satisfaction may encourage your partner to join you in seeking a better sex life, but it just as likely could have little effect or even a negative effect. On the other hand, deciding to improve your sex life for the sake of your partner alone is not enough. Both of you must decide that you want and deserve the pleasures of sexual intimacy, and that each of you as individuals and the bond between you are all worth the effort.

Ideally, your partner is already as seriously committed to creating a more satisfying sex life as you are. If the two of you are reading this book together, you have already completed an important step. But if you haven't yet gotten your partner involved, now is the time to do it—but do it with care and understanding. Since sex is almost always a highly emotional and often threatening subject, putting considerable thought into how you will involve your partner will greatly increase the likelihood of getting full cooperation without making your partner feel threatened. As you would with any important project, develop a plan that anticipates possible problems.

In preparing your plan, keep in mind that people want sex with friends, not with enemies. Although this may seem obvious, it remains basic to sexual happiness. Passion is a powerful emotion, and giving in to it means openly showing your feelings and taking a high risk of not being accepted or of outright rejection. We take such risks only with people we trust, because passion with those we don't trust can be too scary. The development of trust is essential for a satisfying sex life. Most couples create this trust through building a solid friendship. As the friendship grows, so does the belief that one is completely accepted, and the result is a willingness to risk more. This is the key that opens the door to passion.

Even seeking your partner's involvement, reasonable though it may seem, will most likely create some risk and some discomfort for both of you. Ideally, not only will you feel comfortable asking your spouse to participate, but your partner will be enthusiastic about the idea of improving your sexual relationship and trying this or some other way of doing it. However, don't be surprised if your spouse initially resists or even turns a cold shoulder to the whole idea. Talking about sexual concerns and, particularly, getting involved in a specific program to improve one's sex life often raises many obvious and not-so-obvious fears that in turn can create a lot of resistance. In fact, you should probably expect that each of you will encounter some nervousness. But by expecting tension and facing it, you should be able to greatly reduce your own and your lover's sense of risk, and accordingly increase your lover's receptiveness.

A good way to reduce some of this risk and discomfort is to concentrate on the best way to make both of you as comfortable as possible while you seek to involve your partner. Most likely, your approach will be very similar to the way you got yourself ready for your first date, back when you may have been a bit anxious and wanted to make a good impression. To overcome your concerns, you gave extra effort to making sure everything went right. You need to think the same way now to be able to create the right attitude and atmosphere, and in particular to make yourself and your partner feel special.

First make sure that you yourself are willing to risk and that you are willing to help build an atmosphere that makes your partner willing to risk. To do this, you need to feel sufficiently confident that *you* can create a more satisfying sex life. Confidence will help you feel more secure about your sexual future and less likely to lay blame or accept guilt about your sexual past. Ideally, as you become more comfortable with your own sexuality, your interest in the fulfillment of your partner's sexual desires and concerns will increase. Your confidence will help you to show that you accept the uniqueness of your partner, en-

21

courage your partner to risk talking about your sex life together and become willing to improve it with you.

Confidence comes from optimism. Right now, you may find you've gotten physically and mentally out of the mood to really enjoy sex. You may even wonder if you *can* have a satisfying sex life. This doubt is not uncommon, but it definitely is correctable. You may not realize it, but *you already are a great sex partner.* That's right. You were born with the ability to enjoy sex, but for whatever reason, your desires, feelings and performance have become limited. Satisfying sex comes from learning to let your sexual feelings and behavior surface naturally. As you begin to see that you can create the sex life you want, you will find your optimism and your confidence growing. Once you decide that you have the ability and desire to have a great sex life, be optimistic about the future and don't dwell on the frustrations of the past. Build on this optimism, feel your confidence growing, and find yourself more comfortable with sex. (But don't go too fast before you involve your partner or you might create a lot of fear or suspicion. Your partner might even wonder whether you are having an affair.)

As your confidence in your own sexuality grows, you will find it easier to have the same kind of belief in your partner's sexuality. Besides accepting yourself as a sexual person, you must come to accept that your partner is potentially a great lover. Since you may not be enjoying sex much right now, this may seem strange until you realize that your partner may be holding back sexual feelings, desires and performance.

Also, your partner may not know how to be a great lover for *you*. So even though you may not now be receiving what you want sexually (and perhaps never have), that doesn't mean that your partner can't give you what you want. Simply accepting your partner without reservation will lead to a much closer marriage, and your acceptance will allow your partner to risk more and to give more.

As part of your acceptance of yourself and your partner, you will most likely face the question of what is "normal" sex. You may even wonder whether your desires or your partner's desires really are normal. While "normal" has all kinds of definitions, the simplest is that if a sexual activity is acceptable to the two of you, it is normal. What anyone else thinks or does doesn't matter. If it pleases you, it is normal sex for you. If it doesn't, it isn't.

Once you have yourself mentally prepared, you are ready to think about getting your partner involved. Numerous approaches are possible, but it's important to choose one that encourages both of you to feel good about this decision. Be straightforward in explaining what you want, and let your partner see and believe your wish to change. Be honest about your desires and try to put aside past problems. This is not the time to look for sexual arousal—in fact, the more difficulty you are having in your relationship, the more important it will be to avoid any likelihood of arousal.

For this discussion, you'll want to choose a time and place that will allow each of you to talk without feeling pressured. Make sure that you allow enough time to get relaxed and to bring up any issues that are bothering either one of you. Just to be safe, you should probably plan for at least two uninterrupted hours at a time when neither of you has any outside obligations or serious problems on your mind.

Next, choose a special place—a location that's a break from your usual routine, that both of you will like, and that might even create some novelty. Most important of all, find a location that will help each of you relax. Be sure there's enough privacy for talking openly. A candlelight dinner in a restaurant, an isolated spot on the beach or in a park, a pleasant automobile drive or a walk through a scenic area of town—these could be what you're looking for. The more difficulty the two of you are having getting along, the more important a comforting and relaxing setting. By choosing a place with no sexual associations, you will be more able to discuss your hopes openly without the setting arousing threatening feelings. No matter how good your relationship is, *don't* use the bedroom as your place for discussion.

After deciding when and where, tell your partner that you would like to set aside a couple of hours just for the two of you to share some pleasant time together. Avoid discussing your plans in any more depth. If your partner asks questions, simply say that you would like more time together—the way it was when you first started dating. Feel free to change the time or place if a better idea comes up.

When you meet for your special time together,

try to make each of you feel as comfortable and as special as you can. By being comforting and caring and giving real attention to whatever your partner may be talking about, you will make your partner feel important. Again, you may want to think back to what worked when you first started seeing each other. You might want to reminisce, dance, listen to music, indulge in small talk—do whatever is right for the two of you. When you both feel comfortable, simply say how special he or she is and that you would like to bring more pleasure to your romantic times together. You can then say that you would like to use this book to help you create more of the romance and sexual pleasure that you want. Make it clear that because this is something you'd be doing together, the decision to participate will come from both of you.

Focus on encouraging your partner and being honest about the rewards you hope to get. Show your optimism and excitement as you explain the importance of improving your love life. Avoid old problems and reasons for them and, especially, avoid blaming your partner or yourself for problems in the past. Instead, emphasize your hopes for a mutually satisfying romantic and sex life and for the joys you envision for you both. Focus, and focus intently, on building trust through expressing your feelings of friendship.

After you have opened the door to discussing your sexual desires, encourage your partner to share his or her ideas. Take turns sharing your dreams of what romance should be—from daily touching and kissing to romantic celebrations to mad passionate love-making. Finally, encourage your partner to discuss getting involved in this program or any other.

Watch out for the urge to say that your partner is responsible for problems or the urge to blame yourself. On the other hand—and this is especially important—learn to be accepting and uncritical of your own and your partner's ideas, feelings and desires, no matter how different or unusual those may seem to you.

If either of you becomes bogged down in figuring out why a problem exists, just remind yourselves that it does not matter; all that matters is that the two of you have a rewarding plan for creating the sex life you each desire. You need only to determine where you are now and decide to use this plan to get where you want to be. *All the mistakes of the past are in the past and should be forgiven.* Developing this acceptance will pay off immensely, not only now but for the rest of your life.

As you talk, don't be surprised if a wide variety of feelings come to the surface—feelings that range from excitement to anger to sadness to passion. All of them are normal and should be expected. In particular, don't be surprised if you feel much closer and extremely tender and passionate. But if you decide to make love, don't be surprised if it doesn't go very well. No matter how close you feel at this moment, remember that it takes time to alter a sexual relationship that you have spent years creating.

At this point you can't expect miracles. All you really want now is a commitment from both of you.

And that commitment includes not only to work together on your sexual relationship, but to treat each other with more care and respect. This is when you draw on the memories of the best times, the good times and the friendship that has held you together this far.

CHAPTER 5

Courting

WHEN you first started dating, you probably wanted only to show your best and see your lover's best. You enjoyed a period of happiness and anticipation without concern for life's petty routines and drudgery. As you both grew more and more attracted to each other, you managed to overlook your lover's shortcomings, and just took pleasure in being with each other. When you became sexually intimate, the excitement may have made every part of sex memorable.

Much of that excitement was due to the novelty of the new relationship. You probably each made an extra effort to make your time together special. You often prepared ahead of time to make yourself and the setting as close to perfect as possible. Maybe you phoned or sent some little reminder to heighten the anticipation. When you were together, you paid extra attention to your new lover and did things that you knew both of you would enjoy. Looking back now, none of these things by themselves may seem very important, but as a whole they meant a lot to each of you.

This is the time to revive that kind of attention to yourself, your lover and your surroundings. Making simple changes in your appearance, your behavior and in the atmosphere for your love-making will build your excitement and your sexual desire. Extra effort now will pay off many times over in the future.

Appearance

Sexual confidence begins with feeling good about your body. Very few of us look anything like the Miss Americas, movie stars, body builders or athletes that are paraded in front of us as ideals to imitate. As we look at these outstanding specimens we need to remember that they earn great sums of money because they *don't* look like the rest of us. We imperfect types must learn to accept ourselves as we are and get the most out of what we have.

It is especially important to accept yourself as you are and the way you look right now. Most of us have things about our appearance that we wish could be different. Some of them we can change and some of them we can't. The ones we can't change, we have to learn to accept the way they are. Even the things we can change may call for more effort than we want to put out right now. It may sound easier said than done, but you have to remind yourself that you are the person that you are, and that for anybody else to accept you as you are, you have to begin by accepting yourself.

There may be some things about your appearance that you'd like to and can change. Make plans to change these things, but don't get yourself geared up to do the impossible. If you are starting to feel your years, take your age and health into consideration. A fifty-year-old person is not likely to have the firm body of a twenty-year-old, but a fifty-year-old can certainly be an attractive fifty-year-old. Do what you can now to feel more confident about yourself and your appearance, but be realistic and kind to yourself.

Start out by taking an honest look at yourself—your hair, clothes and general appearance—in a full-length mirror. If you find yourself attractive (and especially appealing) you're one jump ahead of most people. However, if you don't find that, now is the time to stop procrastinating and follow through with any reasonable plans you have for becoming sexier. Once you believe that you're sexy, it will be much easier to act and feel that way.

Feeling attractive and radiating that feeling is much easier if you look and feel in shape. Having a perfect body is not necessary, but having a body that you feel good about gives you an extra lift. If you find that you want to tone up, start an exercise program you enjoy and will be likely to continue. You might want to set aside fifteen minutes every other day to devote to your body, or take a brisk long walk every evening. If you need moral support, join an exercise or aerobics class. Whatever you do, be sure it's what *you* want. Physical fitness will not only make you healthier, but can also make you look and feel radiant.

Dressing attractively will take you one step further. Take a close look at your wardrobe. Make sure that your clothing displays an attractive, confident person. This doesn't mean that your clothes need to be fancy or flashy; it just means that they should be an extension of you rather than a restriction. Bring out any special clothes that you used to wear for a night on the town or a quiet intimate time but have stashed away in your closet. If either of you finds that your wardrobe is lacking, splurge on something new that makes you feel good and attractive. You will both find it well worth the time and expense to set aside time to go shopping and try on clothes that both of you find appealing. Be bold. Choose evening wear that feels right for you, lounge wear that increases your sexual confidence and excites your imagination and enthusiasm. Ignore the fashion experts unless you agree with them. Select clothes that make *you* feel good when you wear them.

The right hairstyle and accessories can make a big difference in how you look and feel. (Even a man who thinks this advice is solely for women should take a good look at his face in the mirror.) If either of you has been wearing the same hairstyle, eyeglass frames or jewelry for a long time, you may find that you want to make a change; adding a little freshness to your looks can add a lot of spirit to romance. If you find your hairstyle or color could use some updating, experiment until you find a look that you like. Make sure your eyeglasses compliment your skin tones, facial shape and personality. Both of you can pull out your jewelry and try on some of the favorites that have been put aside. Men may have hidden away favorite watches, cuff links, tie clasps, or whatever. Women will probably find a good afternoon's worth of old memories in their jewelry boxes. Women might also want to learn new make-up skills from an expert (every large department store has one) or learn about coordinating make-up with clothing.

Although personal attraction usually begins with the visual, don't overlook other senses. Enhancing your natural scent, for example, can have a dramatic effect. Most people's natural body scents are attractive, and with perfumes, colognes and aftershave you can highlight your own aroma. Find a combination that catches your attention. To further heighten your sensuality, don't forget the sense of touch; do what you can to make touching you a delightful experience.

Atmosphere

Atmosphere sets the stage for passion and sex. Yes, a passionate moment can occur anywhere and at any time, but why not help ignite the fire? In the right setting, the stresses of daily life quickly evaporate, and an air of anticipation heightens sexual desires and passion.

While dating, couples often spend more time thinking about the mood they want than they spend on the date. They may agonize about making sure they choose the right restaurant, the right clothes, the right conversation. But, as time goes by and this emphasis on making everything perfect dwindles, they often, without realizing it, begin to take each other for granted sexually and romantically.

Taking the time to create the right atmosphere will pay off as much now as it did years ago. Choose several places that you can get to easily to escape from the daily stress and strain of life—convenient places, not the ones you can visit only rarely or on vacations. You might think of various types of places for different types of moods, occasions or times of day. Find a special place where you can leisurely stroll: a secluded woods, a beach or a city street for window-shopping. Check out romantic spots where you can just sit and relax, or restaurants or nightspots where you can snuggle. Think about a weekend hideaway. In any case, recalling places where you used to go will give you some ideas, while exploring new places should be both fun and exciting.

Creating the right atmosphere at home is a must. Since most romance, sexual anticipation and sexual activity occur there, you need to have an atmosphere conducive to peace and romance. Take a good look at your home. Are the rooms that you use for intimate moments the kind of romantic setting you enjoy? If they're not, use your imagination to create the mood you want. This doesn't mean an expensive overhaul or major redecorating; often a few small changes in color or lighting can make all the difference. Planning these changes can be as exciting as the changes themselves.

Begin with the basics: comfortable furniture or

pillows for snuggling; a soft rug to lie on; lighting that can be dimmed as you don't need it. Your bedroom should be the easiest and the most fun to work on. Large fluffy pillows, colorful new sheets and a cozy bedspread can do wonders.

Finally, think about the frills. If you like music, choose something new that you find romantic or dig out some old favorites to conjure up memories. Burn scented candles for a soft glow and for fragrance. Find some bright flowers for cheer and color. Keep a bottle of your favorite beverage ready so that you can toast special occasions. Prepare a snack plate ahead of time for nibbling. Turn down the lights. Put on the music. Build a fire. As you can see, a little planning and imagination can do wonders for romance.

Romance

For couples in a new love, even the simplest activities are wonderful. Although they usually try to find something that both will enjoy, being together is their most important concern. Free time is often spent just cuddling on a couch or walking and holding hands. They enjoy quiet times together by sharing experiences and intimacies.

Their positive attitude is wonderful to see. They exhibit a zest for life and a contagious optimism that everything will turn out for the best. Their every word and action show support for one another. Never thinking about changing the other, they not only accept but encourage each other to be themselves.

The romantic and sexual pleasure of this new love can last a lifetime. While the high intensity of a new love naturally cools with time, the pleasure need not. The bonds forged in the heat of a new love become the foundation for a life-long marriage. The difference is that in a new love, good times just seem to happen. In a lasting love, the good times, including sexual pleasure, need the care and thought we would use to preserve and protect anything precious.

Unfortunately, as we go from a new love to a life-long love, we often fail to give the marriage the care and attention it needs. As work, family and hobbies crowd into our lives, little by little we give up many of the simple activities that once meant so much to us. At the same time, we fall into a rut as far as sex is concerned. Rather than giving it our complete attention, we now accept it as one more ritual of married life.

Instead of letting sex become routine, make it an event to savor. Remember that much of the closeness and fun of sex begins long before you get to the bedroom. For many, the anticipation of sex is as exciting as the act itself.

Reviving your sex life calls for creativity and persistence, but by making simple changes in your day-to-day living you will see immediate and rewarding differences—in yourself and in your marriage. Make the changes in your own personal way, and a whole new sensuality will begin to surface.

Get your partner involved. Discuss how you can put at least a little more romance into the time you spend together. This romance needn't be elaborate, just enough to add a bit of freshness. Recall some favorite times in the past and what made them so special—the humor, the fun, the excitement and the closeness. Look through photo albums and souvenirs to recall some of your happiest moments. Let your memories help you recapture those special feelings and enjoy them all over again.

Put more romance into your everyday living. Give your partner a loving hug and an affectionate kiss when you meet. Hold hands when you're walking. Don't forget the cards, flowers, small gifts and phone calls. Show that little extra courtesy such as opening doors, helping to carry packages, or assisting with coats. Don't forget that everyone appreciates a thank-you or a pat on the back. Thanking your lover for thoughtful and gracious acts can make all the difference in the world. Don't hide your appreciation.

Be positive and open-minded. Your expectations of fun and excitement will become a self-fulfilling prophecy. Put a little extra enthusiasm into whatever you do; push aside your cautions and try new things that you normally might have avoided. As you free up your thoughts, you will find that you can actually enjoy many new activities. At the same time, give your lover extra freedom to do the same.

Openly show your pleasure in being with your lover. Most important, be sure to smile and touch. Nothing is nicer than being greeted with an accepting smile. The more you get into the habit of openly displaying your pleasure and warmth, the easier it will be to genuinely unveil your affection. A welcoming smile often speaks louder than words, and touching often speaks the loudest. Give a hug or caress that says, "I love you."

No matter how expressive smiles and hugs are, words communicate the essence of a relationship. Conversation that is positive, fun and complimentary is conducive to passion. Avoid the urge to complain or dwell on the negative. If you need to get back on track, take an objective look at your conversations and make sure they involve more than complaints. Going back to the basics is a good way to turn your conversations around. Talk about topics you both enjoy. Pay a little extra attention to your partner's problems, stories, feelings and desires. Be supportive, and for heaven's sake avoid the urge to mold your partner into something different than he or she is.

Finally, begin to stretch your sensual imagination. Curl up some evening with a sensually stimulating book or magazine. Consider going to a romantic or erotic movie. And don't be surprised if you and your lover have completely different preferences. Men are more likely to be turned on by visual stimulation such as X-rated movies or provocative pictures, while women tend to be stimulated more by their own imaginations as they read or think about romance. No matter what you choose, make a mental note of what activities, behavior, clothing and personal styles you yourself find sensuous and exciting.

Reviving this romantic excitement is a great way of setting the stage for intensifying your love-making. Learning to appreciate your partner more and to show this appreciation will encourage both of you to put more into your marriage. Building friendship and romance into your marriage will make sex more enjoyable. As your pleasure increases, you will want to be more physically involved, more emotionally involved and more eager to keep the spiral going upward.

Celebrate! Buy a bottle of champagne to proclaim the revival of your friendship and romance. Then move on to your sex education class.

CHAPTER 6

A School for Pleasure

THIS is a school like no other school. There are no grades, no tests, and no last-minute cramming. Your homework *should* be pleasure and your new skill *will* be pleasure. After all, this is a school for pleasure—sexual pleasure.

The most satisfying sexual relationships are those that offer pleasure and excitement at each level of intimacy. In this course, you will have seven assignments, each at an increasing level of sexual intensity and excitement. Each assignment will help you learn or relearn the skills of friendship, trust and romance. The result will be a better marriage and a better sex life.

You'll begin this course, as you would with any school subject, with the introductory levels first. You'll start by making sure that you are each completely comfortable with your own and your lover's nakedness and as you find pleasure and comfort with this, you will gradually advance to more and more intimate sexual contact.

For each assignment you will have specific instructions to practice a particular sexual activity. Classes in this school will be thirty-minute practice sessions that you will schedule as often as you like. The purpose of your practice sessions is simply to enjoy the activity without letting it make either of you uncomfortable, or practicing as long as you need until you both are comfortable. Although the instructions will be specific, you can feel free to add your own personal touches. When you are able to enjoy each assigned activity without discomfort for two consecutive sessions, you move on to the next, more advanced, level.

For each assignment, you will have only as many practice sessions as it takes for both of you to feel satisfied. So while you can breeze through the assignments you find easy, you can spend as much time as you need on the others. You set your own pace. Alternative assignments are available at each level in case you are having trouble. When you finish one assignment, you skip any alternatives you don't need and go on to the next level.

You'll think of many ways of doing each assignment. By choosing the ways that are fun for you, you'll want to practice more and you'll advance more quickly. Success in each practice session is simply enjoying being with your partner for a half-hour.

Scheduling Classes

Attending classes in this school will be just like dating. The two of you will set aside specific times just to enjoy being together. When you were dating, you probably decided to be together on a Saturday afternoon to enjoy some activity together, such as a concert. Although you may not have discussed it, you probably thought to yourself that you would also enjoy some level of physical intimacy together. Here you will do the same thing, but the physical intimacy is openly decided ahead of time.

Scheduling your practice sessions in advance gives you the opportunity to treat this time and yourselves as special—just like you did when you were dating. Scheduling allows the two of you to plan activities that you both will enjoy and to make arrangements for the time to be uninterrupted. Scheduling also gives you the chance to make the sessions a little more special by using your imagination to get yourselves ready, physically and mentally, and creating a romantic atmosphere. Most important, you can show how much you value your partner and your sex life just by being ready on time and ready to begin.

Although you may be thinking that sex ought to be spontaneous, you ought to remember that a lot of sex is scheduled and a lot of planned sex is great. If you think about it, you may even agree that a lot of sex that appears spontaneous is really scheduled—we have all made special plans at times to create a romantic atmosphere, and even though sex may not have been directly discussed, we knew (or at least hoped) that sex would be the outcome. Keep in mind that great sex results from the ability to make each of you feel special, and it is often much easier to create this feeling of being special by planning ahead. When couples find that they can easily enjoy sex by planning ahead, they quickly learn that they can use the same skills to enjoy sex spontaneously.

In this school for sexual pleasure, you will make the most progress in the shortest time by making a schedule and sticking to it. Successful scheduling requires you to make several important decisions now.

You first need to decide if you want to continue your normal sex lives outside of your scheduled sessions. Most sex counselors suggest that all sexual contact, except for the specific assignments and for normal hugging and kissing, be discontinued. They suggest this because having unrestricted sexual activity may lead to the continuation of old habits rather than the solid building of new ones. In short, unrestricted sexual activity may slow down your progress. However, one or both of you may not even want to participate in this school at all if you have to stop all other sexual activity. If both of you are not willing to temporarily give up unrestricted sexual activity, you may want to consider setting aside time for unrestricted sexual activity in addition to having the scheduled sessions. This strategy should still allow you to progress, but most likely not as quickly as limiting yourselves to the assignments. The decision is yours as to how quickly you want to progress. Agree now on whether you want to have unrestricted sexual activity in addition to the scheduled sessions or not.

42

Agree also on the number of half-hour practice sessions you are going to have each week. Remember that your half-hour sessions could easily take an hour when you include the time needed for preparing yourself and the location. Most couples find two to three sessions a week the most practical and realistic. Make sure you plan at least one session a week, but try no more than one a day. In any case, when deciding how many sessions to schedule, choose a number that is convenient and realistic for both of you. Whatever pace you choose, make sure you can stay with it. The best schedule is one that is fast enough to keep you both interested and involved, but slow enough that you can comfortably find the time. Generally, the more sessions you have in a given period of time, the faster your sex life will improve.

Sit down with a calendar and schedule your sessions for next week. Think about what hours of the day will be the most convenient, keeping in mind that you would like them to be at times when you can be as relaxed and alert as possible. Make sure that you choose times that will keep the likelihood of being distracted or interrupted to a minimum. For some, the best time will be at night after the children are asleep. For others, it will be in the early morning before your minds and bodies have become involved in the day's activities. If your kids are a little older or if you have a parent who loves to babysit, Saturdays or Sundays may be good choices.

If you find that every day next week is filled with work, family, friends, PTA, church, clubs, hobbies, sports, aerobics and TV, then you may have just learned what one of your problems is: you are not giving your relationship and love life the priority they need. Although all those other activities may be important, you haven't allowed yourselves enough time to be together as a couple.

Mark the planned practice sessions on a calendar that both of you use, and remind each other of them during the week. Avoid delaying or cancelling any practice times, but by all means add or extend sessions whenever the two of you want to. Try to have at least two hours' advance notice before adding an extra session. If you don't *both* want to have an extra or longer lesson, don't try.

Now that you've agreed on your schedule for the coming week, be sure to stick to it even if it isn't quite as convenient or if you find that you're not as relaxed or eager as you had hoped. Even if you are not "in the right mood," begin each session on schedule. Naturally it's always nice to be in the right mood, but it isn't necessary. In fact, as you begin to enjoy the session and look forward to the pleasure to come, you will probably notice that you seem to get in the right mood without trying.

As the last step in the preparation of your weekly schedule, give a lot of thought to where the sessions will be. Choose places that are warm, comfortable, quiet and private. At first you will most likely want to have your sessions in the convenience and comfort of your home, probably in your bedroom. As you grow more courageous and creative, you may want to try other places. Consider a hot tub for an hour, a motel room for a night or a secluded inn for a weekend. But for your first assignment, leave this decision until you have received the details.

Finally, choose a time to get together each week to plan your schedule for the following week. Try to keep to the same schedule or at least the same number of sessions each week. The most important thing is your commitment to keeping up with the schedule as well as possible.

A workable schedule is *absolutely essential*. Schedule problems can be very discouraging and are the most common reason why couples quit before they've really gotten started. If you have trouble making and keeping your schedule, be reasonable with yourselves and try again. If you have unrealistically scheduled too many practice sessions in a week, just cut back the number. Whenever you have difficulty scheduling practice times for one week, take those problems into account when scheduling for the following week. If one partner has not kept to the agreed plan, he or she should be the one to make the first proposal for the next week. Once you become successful at scheduling, you can always add more sessions.

If you continue to have scheduling difficulties, you probably have not gotten enough pleasure from your assignments. Think of ways (such as a romantic or sexually arousing movie for your home VCR or having your session in an erotic setting) to make the sessions more important.

Think of scheduling as a way to reaffirm your commitment to the sex life you want. As your assignments grow more and more pleasant you will probably find yourselves wanting to practice more. As you are learning to enjoy the sessions, you will be developing the ability to add later the spontaneity and variety that you have always hoped for from sex.

The Practice Sessions

Now for the heart of the matter: the practice sessions, which should be the best part of your day. They should be seen not as an abrupt change from daily living, but as an intensification of it. The sessions are simply a time for the two of you to concentrate on enjoying being together. They should be fun. They should be filled with caring and closeness, and as you progress, greater and greater physical pleasure. The sessions will help you find sexual comfort and sexual pleasure.

Comfort is the key to sexual pleasure. This means feeling comfortable with your own sexuality as well as feeling comfortable with your lover. As you enjoy sustained periods of sexual intimacy without discomfort, feelings of closeness, love, pleasure and excitement will all become a natural part of your intimacy.

As you begin the practice sessions, perhaps only one of you may not be enjoying sex as much as you'd like. As the sessions take place, however, each partner is likely to encounter moments of discomfort. Change itself can be uncomfortable. Comfort is achieved by learning to quickly recognize and eliminate both physical and emotional discomfort as soon as it arises.

The sessions will help you develop comfort at increasing levels of sexual intimacy and intensity.

You will be learning to enjoy each assigned activity without feeling any discomfort or, if you do feel it, acknowledging it and working at eliminating it. It's important *not* to focus on sexual excitement or orgasm. By concentrating instead on *comfort*, the pleasurable, natural sexual functioning of your body will gradually emerge and increase on its own.

Sustained comfort for both partners while participating in an assigned activity is the sign that it's time to advance to the next step. One partner may have difficulty getting comfortable at one stage while the other may experience more discomfort at an entirely different stage. Don't worry, this is common.

The practice sessions themselves are only thirty minutes long. Depending on your desires, preparation for them can last from a few minutes to several hours. Learning to use both the preparation and session time to make each of you feel comfortable and special is what you're after.

Preparation for the Class

For too many couples, sex is as much fun as balancing a checkbook, which leads to sex being nothing more than aerobics for two. As couples begin to add more pleasure to their love-making, sex can take on much more meaning: more love, caring and fun. Making sex *fun* is another key to turning a disappointing sex life around. Preparing for sex can add to the fun and can be great fun in itself.

You prepare for each session by carefully reading the assignment. At least several hours before the scheduled session time, make sure that you both understand the instructions. Think about how each of you would like to complete the assignment and add your own personal touches. Agree on what you'd like to do during the upcoming session. Instead of choosing one person's ideas or even compromising, try to find a plan that includes what both of you would like to do.

When you decide what you'd like to do during the practice session, decide if you'd like to spend some time together before the session or just meet at the agreed-upon place at the agreed-upon time. Occasionally, plan a stroll, an intimate dinner, dancing or a movie as a prelude to your session.

Once you have your general plans outlined, spend a few minutes discussing the specifics. If you will need any special items (such as massage oil) for the practice session, decide who will get them. If you need or want to create a special atmosphere or simply get your session site ready, decide what will be done and who will do it. Finally, decide if you need to make any special preparations so that your session won't be disturbed. Decide now who will make arrangements for the kids, unplug the ever-demanding telephone, and do whatever else needs to be done. You may even want to keep a list of possible interruptions, so that you can avoid any obvious distractions. A little planning here will help you avoid annoying distractions during the sessions.

Whether you plan to do something special ahead of time or not, prepare for each session as if you were going on a date. Get yourself ready and plan some special things that make you and your partner feel good.

Get yourself ready mentally. Find some activity (such as taking a candlelight bath, reading an arousing novel or magazine, watching a movie or taking a nap) that will get you in the mood. Above all, give yourselves the time and permission to forget about work, the kids and whatever else you have on your minds.

Get yourself ready physically. Spend some time before each session making yourself appealing to both yourself and your lover. Relax in a warm, peaceful bath. Splash on your favorite cologne. Put on a sensuous outfit. In short, let yourself look and feel sexy.

Finally, try to do some little things for each practice session that let your partner know he or she is special—a card, flowers, candy, a pint of ice cream or an unexpected phone call would be nice. As part of showing your partner that he or she is special, be on time, ready to go. Being there, but not being ready, is not enough.

The Class

We can't say it too often: *Your most important task throughout this school is to become and stay comfortable*. Simple as this may sound, it may not always be that easy. We all know that getting comfortable, trusting our most intimate thoughts and feelings to another person, can be a very difficult thing to do, even with someone we love. It can be done, though. Anyone can rebuild a sexual relationship, step by step, by gradually increasing the trust, the intimacy, the excitement and the love. The following instructions tell you how.

PARTICIPATE IN THE ASSIGNED ACTIVITY

Begin each practice session at the agreed-upon time. During the session, simply participate in the assigned activity for the full thirty minutes. Follow the instructions as closely as possible, but add your own touches to make them more pleasurable for the two of you. Focus on enjoying the activities of the moment without anticipating problems. Feel free to extend any session for as long as you like, assuming you both agree to it.

LEARN TO RECOGNIZE DISCOMFORT AS SOON AS IT ARISES

In order to create comfort, you must be able to recognize and get rid of any discomfort. Generally, discomfort is defined as any unpleasant physical or psychological feeling or response. Your own definition of discomfort will be personal and may vary from time to time. For instance, you might feel nervous or afraid about how you will act or your partner will act. You could feel up tight, edgy, anxious or even angry. You might think you're going too fast and are being pressured to perform, or even question whether you want to participate in the activity at all. Even if you're able to take part in an activity without a great deal of discomfort, you might still be feeling guilty, ashamed or even disgusted. Sometimes you may feel discomfort from the environment, such as the temperature, lighting or an uncomfortable bed. Discomfort can also arise from an action, such as stroking or massaging too hard. Your physical position may not be to your liking. Naturally, there may be times when your mind and interest are somewhere else.

Many people encounter difficulties simply because they limit their definition of discomfort. Just keep in mind that discomfort is anything that causes uneasiness. The following is a fairly complete definition, but you might want to add to it.

- Feeling anxious, tense, nervous, afraid, up tight, edgy or angry;
- Feeling too hot, too cold or having any other form of physical discomfort;
- Feeling guilty, ashamed or disgusted;
- Feeling rushed or pressured;
- Not wanting to participate in the suggested activity;
- Feeling an uncontrollable desire to participate in a sexual activity that has not yet been assigned.

ACKNOWLEDGE THE DISCOMFORT IMMEDIATELY

Signal your partner the moment you feel that things are not quite right. This acknowledgement should be, preferably, a simple comment. "I'm uncomfortable" is enough. It's often best not to state the cause unless it's something easily remedied. Too often an explanation can sound like blame.

It's most important to learn to recognize and admit your discomfort as soon as it arises. That way you have the best chance of getting rid of the problem and continuing on with a more pleasurable time. Otherwise, the discomfort will only get worse. The longer it takes to recognize your discomfort, the harder it could become to eliminate it. As time goes on, it could be more stressful to tell your partner what the problem is, especially if you feel reluctant to ask your partner to change. Generally, by acting on a problem as soon as it comes up, you create a more positive and successful atmosphere for dealing with it.

Even knowing this, you still may find it difficult at first to signal discomfort as soon as you feel it. But to avoid unnecessary delay and unresolved discomfort, you have to deal with the discomfort and get rid of it before you go on. Keep in mind that you are working on the foundation of a better sexual relationship. If you build on a shaky foundation the entire structure of your love-making will be shaky.

SUGGEST A SOLUTION

When signaling your discomfort to your partner, suggest a way to eliminate it. _Always make your suggestion a positive comment rather than a criticism. And be sure that the tone of your voice is friendly_.

In most cases, the solution will be obvious to you. For example, if you are feeling cold, you may simply want to say "I would like to close the window," or if your partner is massaging you too hard, you may say "Touch me more softly." Sometimes, you may find that you can't think of a solution to suggest. This is particularly likely if your discomfort is fear or if you are beginning to feel overwhelmed. At these times, simply acknowledging the discomfort should be helpful. Since you have no suggestion at the moment, you may want to consider continuing the assignment without making any changes or taking a short break. No matter what, tell your partner of the discomfort and your desires.

DETERMINE A MUTUALLY ACCEPTABLE SOLUTION

If the solution that you suggest is acceptable to the two of you, that's great. If it is not acceptable to your partner, your partner should suggest an alternative solution. Ideally, this alternative will be acceptable to you. If it is not, the two of you should jointly take your individual desires into account and find a solution that is acceptable to both of you.

ATTEMPT TO ELIMINATE THE DISCOMFORT

After you have agreed upon a solution, act on it. If the discomfort disappears, that's great. If the discomfort persists, you should again acknowledge discomfort and suggest a solution. If no solution seems to work, you might simply try taking a two-minute break.

CREATE AN ATMOSPHERE OF COOPERATION

Even the signaling of discomfort may itself cause

discomfort for you or your partner. All too often, acknowledging discomfort is interpreted as somebody's failure. It's important to remember that signaling discomfort is simply a way to improve the situation and is *not* a criticism of either of you. If you feel uncomfortable when your partner signals discomfort, acknowledge the discomfort the signal has caused *you* and suggest a way your partner can signal discomfort without making you uncomfortable.

If your own signaling of discomfort makes you uncomfortable, be sure to acknowledge *this* discomfort too. This is a common situation that a little attention can remedy. You don't need to suggest a solution, but you do need to accept that it is OK to ask for help, and that as long as you communicate and ask for your partner's help in a positive and friendly way, that's all that matters.

ACKNOWLEDGE COMFORT AND PLEASURE

Let your partner know when you're feeling good. Don't take it for granted that it's obvious. Put your happiness into words or sounds. It will make both of you more comfortable, and will show the progress you're making.

It's even more common for couples not to acknowledge sustained comfort than not to acknowledge discomfort. Words such as "That feels good" are extremely important. Positive statements will not only make each of you feel better, but also help you realize how far you've come. And, as any street-corner philospher will remind you, success breeds success.

If you complete the assigned activity with comfort, that's great. When you are able to comfortably complete two consecutive practice sessions, skip the rest of the chapter and begin the next assignment. If, after three sessions, you still are not able to complete the assignment without discomfort, use the alternative assignments to help you progress.

Rewards for Your Efforts

When couples first start this course, it is not unusual for their sexual desires to be relatively limited. However, as you advance through the various steps, you will become very much aware of the increase in your desires. But until that point, you may need encouragement to continue to practice regularly. We suggest that you regularly reward yourselves *just for trying*.

The practice sessions are absolutely essential. Couples who successfully stick to their scheduled sessions are the ones who reach the sexual intimacy they want. When the sessions are proceeding well, just the good feelings that you get during a session will usually be enough to encourage you to go on to the next one. However, when you're not progressing as fast as you'd like, you can lose interest. At these times, a good reward system for just making the attempt will help you keep moving forward.

Your rewards will be of two kinds. First, there's the psychological reward of feeling good about the overall progress you've made. Whenever you begin to feel that progress is slow, look back to see how far you've come. Second, give yourselves a more tangible treat simply for trying. At the end of every five practice sessions, reward yourselves. The rewards should be based on sessions completed, not on progress.

Three pointers regarding a reward: First, it has to be something you both like; second, it should be of the right value—not so extreme that you can't manage it after it's been earned, nor so common that it's meaningless; third, it should be a treat, not a necessity. Change the reward, of course, whenever you want. Some rewards might be:

- Eating out
- Going to a movie
- Having a candlelight dinner at home or an elegant breakfast in bed
- Exchanging chores
- Buying a bottle of your favorite beer or wine
- Playing a favorite game or sport
- Having a romantic interlude that is not a scheduled practice session.

Abide by two simple rules regarding rewards. Whenever you have earned one, you should receive it. If you have not earned one, it is not fair to receive one.

So decide what your first mutually-agreed-upon reward is to be. Then start earning it by doing your first assignment.

Summing Up the Rules

Following these basic rules will virtually assure success.

- Together, schedule practice sessions and stick to your schedule.
- Treat each session as a special time. Plan to add some fun to each session.
- Get yourself in the mood before each session.
- Tell your partner about both your pleasure and your discomfort. Signal discomfort promptly and suggest a positive way to eliminate it. Don't get into a discussion of the cause of your discomfort, but instead find a solution to increase your pleasure.
- Don't anticipate future problems; enjoy pleasure and comfort *here and now*.
- Be persistent. Repeated practice at getting comfortable, particularly at points in the practice sessions that are difficult for you, will pay off.

You are ready now for your first assignment.

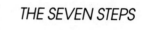
THE SEVEN STEPS

CHAPTER 7

Step 1: Getting to Know You

WHEN we think of sex, we usually think first of orgasm. This emphasis on orgasm, especially when sex is disappointing, is unfortunate, because sex is a lot more. Not that orgasm isn't a fabulous sensation—it is. But orgasm is just one part of an extremely rewarding activity. Sex often begins with a touch, a smile or a friendly word. It includes hugs, kisses and petting, and intercourse. Of course, it's love, passion and great physical pleasure. And it's also fantasies, dreams and memories. Really enjoying love-making means enjoying every stage of sex from the first spark to orgasm to the heavenly feeling afterwards. Learning to enjoy each stage calls for going back to the basics.

Your first assignment is to learn, or more likely

relearn, how to enjoy being together naked. All you need to do during the practice sessions is just feel good being together while undressed. Although it may not seem important, being comfortable together while naked is essential. Once you have this step mastered, you can go on to bigger and better things.

You may be tempted to skip this assignment or rush through it because you have done it so many times before. Sure, you have been naked together many times, but you probably haven't enjoyed it recently in the way suggested here. In the last few years, you probably haven't thought of being together naked as fun or romantic unless you made love along with it. Years ago, you may have had some great times skinny-dipping, playing strip poker or just showering together—the same kind of fun, excitement and freedom you are going to enjoy now.

The first time the two of you were naked together, you may have felt awkward. Because of the newness of the experience each of you was probably cautious about making the correct move. During your practice sessions you may again feel awkward—not because of the newness, but because you are used to rushing through this step. Usually when you are undressed together, it is because you are in the process of making love or going to sleep. This time, just enjoy being naked together without expecting to go any further.

Overcoming any awkwardness and learning to feel totally at ease while completely naked is very important. The best way to combat any uneasiness is to make each practice session special, so give a little extra advance thought to the mood, getting ready, and having something to do that you both will enjoy.

Each of us can visualize a room that radiates intimacy, and that's what you want. You will most likely think of your living room or bedroom, either of which is fine, but if you have a better idea, go for it. Turn down the lights. Maybe you'll want some mood music. If you choose the bedroom, put fresh sheets on the bed. Fluff up several pillows so that you can lean against them, or better yet buy some special pillows just for cuddling. Finally, prepare a snack such as wine and cheese, Coke and popcorn, milk and fresh-baked cookies or whatever the two of you particularly enjoy.

If possible for either or both of you, just before the session take a long sensuous bath. Then put on an outfit that makes you feel sexy, which could be anything from your handsomest evening wear to romantic loungewear. Finally, splash on some cologne (both of you). As you get ready, keep in mind that the sexier you make yourself, the sexier your partner will want to be.

At the designated time for your session undress. Yes, even though you may have taken an hour to put it on, you now have to take it all off. You can choose to undress yourself or let your partner undress you. You might slowly undress over the length of the entire session or completely undress at the beginning. Just select a pace you like and vary the procedure to suit yourselves. You could even play strip poker and take your time taking it off. After undressing (at least partially), start the session by lying facing each other, touching and feeling each other's warmth. Hug and cuddle. Kiss affectionately, but for the time being avoid kissing erotically. Throughout the session, do things you both enjoy. Stretch your imagination. Have fun. You may feel like just cuddling and talking, playing cards or board games, watching TV, or even dancing to some romantic music. Whatever—as long as you stay close and touch each other frequently.

Variety will make your session more fun. Instead of bathing alone before each practice session, spend your whole session bathing together. How about a candlelight bubble bath together, with champagne? Or body-painting each other and then having the fun of washing it off. When you have the time, you could take bathing one step further and rent a hot tub for an hour or two. This will give you privacy as well as a very romantic setting for lying back and getting to know each other again. Don't forget the restriction, though: no sexual caressing or kissing during these sessions. Don't worry, you will begin erotic kissing and caressing soon.

If you find yourself enjoying some aspect of the assignment, comment on it. When you find something about your partner that looks sexy or attractive, say so. You needn't overdo it, and at this stage you may not have too much to say. But keep your mind open for giving compliments. Your partner will certainly appreciate them, and compliments will help each of you feel better—and will pay off manyfold—by the end of the program.

Since this assignment is relatively easy, it gives the two of you a chance to focus on identifying and increasing comfort, while eliminating discomfort. Discomfort, remember, means any physical or emotional uneasiness. This could be feeling chilled, anxious or embarrassed. Recognizing discomfort as soon as it occurs is important if it's going to be eliminated before it becomes disruptive.

Although you may very likely feel sexually stimulated during this assignment, reaching the point of uncontrollable sexual arousal should be included in your definition of discomfort. Keep in mind that the purpose of this assignment is simply for the two of you to learn to get comfortable and stay comfortable just being naked together. Getting more sexually involved during these initial sessions will, unfortunately, delay the establishment of the strong foundation that you're building.

If you feel any discomfort, let your partner know about it right away. All you need to do is say, "I'm uncomfortable." Then it is your responsibility to suggest a way to eliminate this particular discomfort. Don't get into any discussion about the cause of the discomfort. Simply find a solution that is acceptable to both of you. You might suggest changing what you're doing in a way that will increase your comfort, or trying something different that will decrease discomfort. For example, if you feel uneasy while looking at either of your naked bodies, get dressed again and then, when you both feel comfortable, gradually undress completely. If you grow uncomfortable while undressed, you could take a bath instead of playing cards, or you could lie next to each other in a different position, or simply separate and lie apart. Do whatever it takes.

Don't be surprised if acknowledging discomfort at first feels like blaming. Although discomfort is definitely not criticism of either of you, acknowledging it may be hard at first and may make you or your lover uncomfortable. If you feel uncomfortable talking to your partner about a particular concern, let your partner know that too. Similarly, if your lover's acknowledgment of discomfort makes you uncomfortable, admit your uneasiness and try to find a way to get rid of it.

If both of you are successful at eliminating discomfort during the session, continue as long as you like. However, if you are unable to find a way to become comfortable within a few minutes of noticing discomfort, stop the session and do something else. Then try again at the next scheduled time.

Schedule this assignment for three thirty-minute sessions. When you both are able to easily eliminate discomfort during two consecutive sessions, you are ready to move on to Step 2. If you want more time to practice, feel free to schedule as many additional sessions as you like. However, if at any time after the three sessions, you find you aren't progressing as quickly as you would like, read Alternative 1.

Remember that discomfort is any sense of uneasiness. Be sure to signal discomfort, if you feel:
- Anxious, nervous, afraid, up tight, edgy, or angry;
- Too hot, too cold or bothered by any other form of physical discomfort;
- Guilty, ashamed or disgusted;
- Rushed or pressured;

- Compelled to attempt an activity not prescribed or not wanting to attempt what had been prescribed;
- That your body was responding unpleasantly or not at all.

ALTERNATIVE 1

You have acknowledged discomfort that should be gotten rid of before moving on to the next step. This is an encouraging sign, since it shows that you are able to face problems and want to develop ways of getting rid of discomfort and becoming comfortable with your sexuality. Although feeling comfortable with this assignment may take some practice, you will certainly reap the benefits in the long run.

Since you have had difficulty remaining comfortable for thirty minutes, you might try exactly the same things again, but for a shorter time. Instead of planning half-hour sessions, this time schedule three fifteen-minute sessions. If you are successful the first time, lengthen the time for your next session. On the other hand, if fifteen minutes is still too long, try ten minutes or even less. If short time periods aren't the answer, go on to the next alternative.

ALTERNATIVE 2

Even though you have had some problems maintaining comfort for the full practice sessions, your aim is still to enjoy being naked with each other while refraining from caressing or kissing. However, in contrast to previous sessions, this time you will actually try to create the discomfort and then eliminate it.

It is likely that during the practice sessions you have delayed acknowledging discomfort to each other. By recreating the unpleasant situation you will learn to recognize uneasiness sooner and be able to tell your partner more quickly that it exists and how to eliminate it.

As usual, schedule three sessions for this. When the time for the session arrives, begin as you did before. Feel free to undress immediately or, if you prefer, experiment with remaining partially dressed for a while longer before eventually undressing completely. After a few minutes, try to engage in the activity that previously produced discomfort. Since you are trying to create this situation, you will be able to identify and acknowledge the discomfort as soon as it arises. Having identified the discomfort immediately, you should now be able to eliminate it. If you need help in thinking of a solution, discuss the problem frankly and openly. Your partner may be able to suggest a way to reduce the discomfort.

If after trying the above technique for three practice sessions, you are still having difficulty maintaining comfort for two consecutive sessions, read Alternative 3.

ALTERNATIVE 3

One of the best ways to reduce stress is to use your imagination. The technique described here is a simple method that you could find valuable for eliminating many of life's stresses. It involves nothing more than thinking of a pleasant experience whenever something stressful occurs. By focusing on the pleasant experience, the peacefulness of that event will gradually replace the stress of the existing one. Simple though it is, it will help you eliminate discomfort during sexual intimacy or during any stressful time.

Since this technique is one that both of you will find useful, most likely you will both want to learn it eventually. However, if only one of you is having difficulty eliminating discomfort during the practice sessions, maybe only that partner will want to learn it now.

Practice for ten minutes at a time, twice a day or more, the following exercise.

Imagine a very pleasant scene for two minutes, such as lying on a beach after swimming and feeling the warmth of the sun. Try to picture in your mind as many details of the scene as you can, imagining the feelings as if you were actually there. Make the scene feel as real as you possibly can.

As soon as you're able to vividly imagine yourself in the pleasant scene for two minutes, turn off the scene and imagine yourself with your partner during the sessions. Try to imagine the experience of the discomfort, and as soon as you begin to feel it, end the uncomfortable scene and go back to the pleasant one until the discomfort fades and the comfort returns.

Again imagine yourself naked with your partner and again stop this scene when discomfort returns. Finish with the pleasant scene. Do this for ten minutes, at least twice a day.

After two days (at least four sessions with your imagination) schedule three practice sessions of being naked together. If you become uncomfortable, signal your partner. To help reduce your discomfort, create the pleasant scene in your imagination. As soon as you are comfortable, continue with the session. Whenever discomfort returns, bring back the pleasant image. Repeat this process of using your pleasant image to reduce your discomfort as often as necessary for the thirty-minute session. Continue the image session twice daily in addition to the regular practice sessions with your partner.

If, after three attempts you have not been successful for two consecutive sessions, read Alternative 4.

ALTERNATIVE 4

Don't worry about not progressing quickly. Comfort comes with time and practice. Discuss the problems you're having. It's important to be open and frank with each other regarding your comfort and discomfort. Talking it over will help you get rid of the discomfort more quickly.

Since you seem to need extra practice at this stage, the odds are that you have not had enough practice sessions or are not signaling soon enough. Comfort will come with perseverance. Go through this assignment again as if it were the first time. As you continue to practice, use the insight you now have to decrease discomfort, making certain that you signal discomfort *immediately*.

Schedule and hold sessions frequently, discuss your discomfort openly, and use this shared information to help you decrease the discomfort. If it still continues, you may want to consider discussing your discomfort with a professional counselor.

Keep going with what you've begun! This is a time when you may be needing encouragement, so be sure to reward yourselves after every five sessions.

CHAPTER 8

Step 2: Giving and Getting

YOUNG children possess one of life's most precious treasures—the ability to take the simplest situations and turn them into great fun. Give a child a simple block of wood and that child will imagine a boat, a building, an airplane or any number of things that we adults would never think of.

Just as children do, some adults find a lot more fun and play in life than others. Even when things are going bad, they're able to look at the brighter side of life because they've learned how to include this sense of playfulness in everything they do.

Alas, as we grow older, many of us lose this gift; rather than feeling good about the pleasures of life, we tend to become increasingly burdened by our day-to-day responsibilities. Careers and home life consume our attention because we believe we must be serious and productive in everything we do. Pleasure takes a definite second place. We often seem to enjoy life only if we spend a lot of money, drink enough alcohol, or get away from it all on a vacation.

To genuinely enjoy sexual intimacy, we must recapture some of the sense of play of childhood and put aside for a while the seriousness of adulthood. Couples who find sexual fulfillment create a mutual pleasure that temporarily transcends all other experience. Such couples enjoy the intensity of the moment, completely absorbed in giving and accepting pleasure, and having no concern for accomplishing any goals—including orgasm.

Fortunately, creating this pleasure is a skill that can be learned; but unfortunately, our educational systems don't offer courses entitled "The Art of Giving and Receiving Pleasure." While our schools emphasize the development of the skills that can make us rich and successful, they generally ignore the skills for enjoying life. As a consequence, our abilities to enjoy pleasure usually develop haphazardly.

Worse, many of the skills that people acquire to be successful in life tend to conflict with enjoying life's pleasures. Society teaches us to set long-range goals and work hard to reach them. Some of us get the idea that we can't be satisfied until our goals are reached. We often worry and fret about "success," without letting ourselves feel good about our small steps of progress—an attitude that is particularly in conflict with the enjoyment of sex. People who truly enjoy love-making have no goal other than feeling and sharing the joys of the moment.

Besides learning to overemphasize long-range goals, many of us develop other attitudes that limit our ability to share pleasure. We tend to learn either to give or to receive pleasure, so that some of us are better at accepting pleasure, others at giving it. Not many of us are able to enjoy both equally. As a simple example, there are those who prefer preparing a meal for a large get-together and those who prefer eating it. Similarly, many people who enjoy giving gifts feel awkward when receiving them.

Satisfying intimacy requires that each lover be both a generous giver and a willing taker. People who are primarily only one or the other don't enjoy love-making to the fullest. Givers make sure their partner enjoys love-making, but often at the cost of their own pleasure. They may even fake excitement or orgasm so that their partner feels satisfied. Takers, on the other hand, enjoy sex for themselves but miss out on the joys of sharing. To enjoy mutually satisfying sex, you will want to be skilled in giving and taking pleasure simultaneously.

Massage is an effective way of learning to become both a generous giver and a willing taker. The reason it's effective is that it feels good—nothing is more relaxing than enjoying a lengthy sensuous massage. Lying down and allowing yourself to forget all your troubles while your lover rubs every muscle of your body is a wonderful feeling. But no matter how wonderful that may be, don't overlook the other pleasure: giving a massage to your lover. Watching, hearing and feeling your lover enjoy the pleasure you are giving can be just as gratifying as receiving the massage yourself. This is especially true if you as the massager focus on the gentle touching and rubbing while letting all the rest of life's cares fade away.

Massage lets you communicate without speaking. You can show your love, caring and friendship without uttering a word. Through massage, couples learn to develop a comradeship that brings them much closer together. The more you can tune into your partner's pleasure, the more you can share in your partner's experience and express your own pleasure. Often the sensual experience of massage creates a spiritual peace and a true bonding with one's mate. Just as two become joined during sexual intimacy, they can become joined through massage.

Your new assignment is to learn to enjoy giving and receiving a massage. During each practice session, each of you will massage the other. All you need to do is enjoy it. Since massage is most effective when you can relax and open up all of your senses, you will want to pay special attention to creating a peaceful atmosphere. When you schedule your three half-hour sessions, decide for each session which person will receive the first massage and agree on a plan for creating the right environment.

A relaxing atmosphere begins, of course, with your usual preparation, choosing a convenient location where you'll have at least thirty minutes of uninterrupted peace and, if possible, the chance to take a relaxing bath before starting. Add to your preparation by buying some baby oil or a massage lotion that you both like. A small amount of oil will reduce any friction on the skin during a massage. If you prefer, you can make your own massage oil by adding perfume to vegetable oil. If you are concerned about the messiness of oil, you will find that baby oil soaks quickly into the skin, and any excess can be removed with a towel. Warm the oil by warming the container in a pan of water on the stove (before the session) or warming the oil in your hands as you use it, a few drops at a time.

In selecting the right setting, don't limit yourselves to the obvious. Although most couples will choose their bedroom, remember that the person receiving the massage will need to be on a fairly level supportive surface. Indoors, a carpeted floor may be a better location than a bed. If you want to be outdoors, a warm beach or a grassy field would be great, but your back yard or deck would work just as well. No matter what place you choose, provide extra support for the neck, lower back, elbows, knees and ankles of the person receiving the massage. Pillows, blankets and bulky clothes will do the job just fine.

Warmth is an important consideration. Remember that a person being massaged barely moves and can easily feel chilled, so choose a place that is at least 70 to 75 degrees. How about next to a fire or wood stove on a sheepskin rug while sipping hot buttered rum? Wherever you are, make sure the massager's hands are warm. The person receiving the massage may want to remain partially clothed or have a blanket or towel covering any parts of the body not being massaged.

Create an environment that appeals to all of your

senses. Soft lighting will do a lot; a shaded lamp is fine, but candlelight or moonlight are even better. Pay attention to sounds and smells, too. If you are indoors, choose music that is both relaxing and soothing. If you are outdoors, select a place where you can enjoy nature's own symphony. If you both like fragrances, consider scented candles, flowers, incense, perfume or scented massage oils.

Start each session by lying next to each other for a few minutes. When you both feel ready, begin final preparations for the massage. If you are not yet undressed, the first to be massaged should undress at this point. The massager should wear whatever clothes are comfortable. Obviously, if you are in a public place such as a beach, you will want to undress only partially. Remove watches and jewelry so they don't get in the way. After one of you lies down, the massager should see that the recipient is comfortable, with blankets and pillows for warmth and support.

Begin the massage anywhere. Many people especially enjoy being massaged on their faces, backs, legs and feet. *Don't massage or touch the genitals*, though—that's not part of this assignment. Discover which parts of the body your partner particularly enjoys having massaged. When the session is half over, reverse the roles.

During the massage, the partner being massaged needs only to lie there and enjoy it. Pleasure will come quickly. As the massage loosens all of the muscles and as the body relaxes, the mind will grow increasingly tranquil. Worries and concerns will vanish as an all-consuming peacefulness sets in. Slow rhythmic deep breathing—inhaling through the nose and exhaling through the mouth—will make the body and mind relax even faster.

While you're giving the massage, explore the shape and feel of your spouse's body. Mold your hands to fit the contours that your hands are passing over. Avoid any jerky movements or interruptions and maintain steady pressure and speed in your strokes, but do not hesitate to gradually vary them. Once you have made contact with your mate's body, keep the feeling of unity by not losing contact until the massage is completed. Even when you move from one part of the body to another, keep the contact continuous by gliding your hands from one place to the next.

Touching should focus on the muscular and fleshy parts of the body while avoiding the bony parts. In particular, make sure that you massage along the sides of the spine rather than directly on the bones themselves. Try different techniques and pressures to determine what feels best. Start with gentle strokes and gradually increase the pressure. Massage large muscles as if you were kneading bread dough.

Although as massager you'll want to stroke in whatever way you both find most pleasurable, it's usually best to use the full surface of both hands, keeping your fingers together. Generally, you will want both your hands to do the same thing. When you make stroking movements, push towards the heart to increase circulation. Also, keep your stroking rhythmic and symmetrical: if you massage the left side of the body (for example a leg), immediately follow by massaging the right side. Long continuous strokes make it easier for both the massager and recipient to follow the strokes and for the recipient to relax. Whether you are giving or receiving, let your mind follow the hands giving the massage. This helps both partners to relax and develop a sense of closeness.

Massage usually feels best when the pressure slowly increases as the muscles relax. Although considerable pressure can be exerted on large muscles such as those in the thigh, you don't need to be big and strong to give a good massage. Whenever you want to add extra pressure, lean the weight of your body into your hands. Using your hands as an extension of your whole body results in the best massage.

If you would like to learn more about massage, you might want to get a copy of *The Massage Book* by George Downing, which is excellent for learning specific techniques for massaging each part of the body.

During your first two massage practice sessions, keep a dialogue going during the entire session. Although this may at first seem unnatural and even counterproductive, it is valuable for each of you to know what you and your partner enjoy. Talking about your pleasure will help you understand your feelings and help your lover do the things you like best. The person receiving the massage will probably talk more, but it is important that both partners describe their positive feelings while giving and receiving a massage. Let your partner know what you like about the physical sensations. Avoid getting wrapped up in your own thoughts and forgetting to share them.

Communicate your pleasure as accurately and completely as possible. The person receiving the massage may want to say things like "What you're doing really feels good," "I feel so relaxed," or "This feels great!" You might also want to make "ooh's" and "ah's." The partner giving the massage may want to talk about the pleasure of watching and touching, and about the attractiveness of the other's body and skin. In addition, the massager should give particular attention to the pleasure of watching and hearing the recipient's enjoyment. The massager might want to say, "I'm glad you like this," "I can feel your body relax," or "Your skin feels so soft."

In addition to communicating your enjoyment, concentrate on keeping your actions positive, whether you're giving or receiving the pleasure. If you find yourself enjoying something, smile. You'll find that this will make both you and your partner more enthusiastic and confident. Also try to be as flexible as possible in accommodating your lover's wishes. By giving a little extra effort to your partner's enjoyment, you most likely will find the same courtesy given back to you. In developing this readiness to increase each other's pleasure, you will both be enriching your intimacy and the rest of your relationship as well.

While you talk, let your partner know of any discomfort you feel or any suggestions you have for greater pleasure. Even though you may have massaged each other many times before, don't expect your partner to read your mind. Say what you want, but don't complain or nag. Give directions that will tell your partner exactly what to do. Use specific descriptive instructions like: "Rub more to the right," or "I would like to take a break because my fingers are tired," rather than "You're doing it wrong," or "My hands hurt." We all know our likes better than anyone else, and it's our responsibility to tell others in a positive way. As the old song advises, you've got to accentuate the positive and eliminate the negative.

When you express discomfort, don't worry about why the problem exists or let it interrupt. Focus on relieving the discomfort and avoid getting into any underlying reasons for it. All you're interested in is whatever is necessary to restore comfort. As in all sessions, communicate any discomfort promptly, agree on a possible solution without discussing causes and then attempt the solution immediately. If you need to, temporarily stop the massage and just lie next to each other until you are both comfortable again.

At this stage of your learning, sexual arousal should be considered discomfort. The purpose of these massage sessions is not to get either of you sexually stimulated—rather it is for you to learn to get comfortable and remain comfortable while touching or being touched. Strengthening the foundation of your love, trust and pleasure is very important for the steps to come.

You may be surprised after these sessions by how much more of your feelings you can share with your spouse. By hearing yourself acknowledge pleasure and discomfort, you will be able to get more in touch with your body and the sensations that give you pleasure. This will help each of you feel more positive about your body and more in control of the enjoyment the two of you share. Your comments will also make your partner feel good about helping to create this enjoyment. At the same time, you will learn more about the sensations your lover enjoys. You may even be surprised by how much you both are really enjoying massage now that you have accepted it and added it to your sex life.

Schedule three thirty-minute massage sessions. If you'd like to lengthen the sessions, continue the massages as long as both of you want. In the first two sessions, describe your physical sensations as completely as possible. You may have to communicate the same positive feelings or discomfort several times before you are both comfortable with the massaging. Your assignment is to experiment with various ways of increasing comfort. As long as you can easily eliminate discomfort during a session, you have been successful. When you both find that you're really looking forward to the massaging, you may find greater pleasure by trying it in silence. If a recipient has relaxed to the point of falling asleep, that's a compliment to the massager. Gently waken the sleeper after a few moments.

When you both are able to eliminate discomfort during two consecutive sessions, you are ready to move on to Step 3. If you want more time to practice, feel free to schedule as many additional sessions as you like. However, if at any time after the three sessions, you find you aren't progressing as quickly as you would like, read Alternative 1. Regardless of how things are going, don't forget to reward yourselves.

Remember that discomfort is any sense of uneasiness. Here's the list of things you need to be aware of during the massage sessions. Signal discomfort, if either of you feels—

- Anxious, nervous, afraid, up tight, edgy or angry;
- Too hot, too cold, or bothered by any other form of physical discomfort;
- Guilty, ashamed, or disgusted;
- Rushed or pressured;
- Compelled to attempt an activity not prescribed or not wanting to attempt the activities that had been prescribed;
- That your body was responding unpleasantly or not at all.

ALTERNATIVE 1

Since you apparently had difficulty in completing two consecutive practice sessions with comfort, schedule a special session for the specific purpose of discussing the problems you're having. Make certain that you have been recognizing and acknowledging discomfort as soon as it arises. Be open and frank with each other regarding the massaging and actions that each of you finds comfortable and uncomfortable. If you encounter difficulties in discussing this, you could each make a list of things you like about the massage and things you dislike. Then, develop together specific plans on how to eliminate these problems and add pleasure. Now, start this assignment over and continue having massage sessions as long as you are progressing. Perseverance and tolerance should lead to the comfort you desire.

If you can't seem to overcome the discomfort, you might want to consider seeing a professional counselor.

SPECIAL SECTION FOR WOMEN

If you would like to have more exciting and more frequent orgasms, there's an easy technique you can learn. Practicing it will take only a few minutes of your day, and it will add a whole new dimension to love-making. You just need to do a simple exercise in addition to the regular practice sessions. The exercise will make sex more pleasurable for you and more rewarding for your lover. Benefits usually include:

- Increased sensations of pleasure in your genital area;
- Greater sexual excitement for both of you;
- Easier orgasms for you through intercourse;
- Stronger vaginal muscles.

The exercise is designed to strengthen the muscles of the pelvic floor, the pubococcygeus muscle in particular. This is a major muscle that runs from the pubic bone to the tailbone and forms part of the pelvic floor. It lies on both sides of the urethra, vagina and anus. During sexual stimulation, the contraction of this muscle helps to excite you and bring you to orgasm. Like all muscles, it needs regular exercise to maintain good tone. For a noticeable change in the strength of these pelvic-floor muscles, you'll need at least two to three weeks' practice and generally about three months for a maximum gain.

The pubococcygeus muscle is relatively easy to locate since it is the muscle that stops urine flow. You can feel it by starting to urinate and stopping your flow (although it may take several trials before you actually feel the muscle contracting). After you have successfully identified this muscle, try to pull it tight when you are not urinating. If you put your finger into your vagina, you will be able to feel the muscle contracting.

To strengthen your pubococcygeus muscle and keep it in good tone later on, exercise it regularly by alternately contracting and relaxing it. Here's how to do it:

1. Pull it tight as if you were stopping urine flow.
2. Hold it tight for four seconds.
3. Release it for four seconds.

Three times a day, contract and release this muscle ten times. You can do it anywhere: while working, shopping or even waiting for a red light to turn green. Many women find it convenient to do this before getting out of bed in the morning, at suppertime and at bedtime. Continue on a daily basis for at least the next three months, and then on a regular basis (say two days weekly) in order to assure that the muscle stays in shape.

Start the exercise now and do it daily. This little bit of effort now will pay off later—specifically, in Steps 5, 6 and 7, but in years to come as well.

CHAPTER 9

Step 3: Lighting the Fire

MOST animals perform some sort of courting ritual before mating—some simple, some very elaborate. For people, it's possible to have sexual intercouse without any presexual activity at all, and even though the act can result in orgasm, it usually leaves one or both partners feeling cheated. Just as food tastes better when you're hungry, so is sex more satisfying if it's something you really want and are really ready for.

We have many names for this act of getting ready to make love—necking, petting, making out, sparking, getting worked up, watching the submarine races—the words vary depending on when and where you grew up. You probably did your fair share of this presexual activity as a teen-ager or in the early dating stages of your relationship. Unfortunately, after marriage many couples seem to forget about those pleasures. Common complaints are: "You never hug me any more." "You never rub my neck any more." "Why don't you ever kiss (hold, nuzzle, blow in my ear) any more?" All the arts that used to be practiced for hours on the living-room couch, at the drive-in movie or while parked on a dead-end road are the prelude to sexual activity.

Reviving this courting ritual keeps romance a-live. Tender touches and sensuous kisses gently arouse the natural passion within each of us. This passion begins with the message that we are wanted. We can say to ourselves, "My partner wants me and me alone. I'm not just an available body." Even if we begin with no sexual arousal, the courting ritual slowly releases our sexual juices. Each lover gradually shuts off thoughts of everything else as the runaway feelings of sexual rapture take over.

Here is your chance to re-experience those mem-orable teen-age pleasures of necking. Yes, that's right. It's time to do some good old back-seat-of-the-car heavy necking. Teen-agers certainly enjoy it, and there is no reason why adults can't. When you were in high school, you probably relished it so much that you did it wherever and whenever you could find the chance. There were probably times when you became so en-grossed in the passion of the moment that getting home on time became a problem. If it was that much fun back then, you certainly should try it again. It may be even more fun now.

Necking, without the pressure or expectation that it will lead to sexual intercourse, allows you to recognize those sensations that you and your partner find especially pleasurable and those that make you feel uncomfortable or sexually turned off. As you get into it, you will find yourself gradually becoming engrossed in the passion of the moment. Don't be surprised if once again you become so totally wrapped up in your necking that you lose all track of time. This time, however, it will be the parents getting home late rather than the kids.

Take some extra time to plan for this assignment. Creating just the right atmosphere is probably even more important now than for the preceding practice sessions. Since this is the first assignment to deliberately ignite your sexual spark, you will want to make every effort to be in the mood. Necking can be fun and necking can be romantic, but you have to be ready.

Atmosphere really counts when you want to get in the mood for a little passion. A simple way to do this is to talk together about the beginning of your relationship. A woman and man discovering each other is always fun and we can all enjoy reliving the memories. Bringing back memories will build a solid bond while setting an upbeat tone for the sessions. Discuss the romantic times you had and how you felt. In particular, recall the early activities of your courting. You will probably remember that you necked wherever and whenever you had the chance. Think about exactly what you did: Where? When? Most important, recall the fun and excitement when the two of you first started dating. Finally, think about what made it so special.

Choose a place that will encourage some of those old memories or will build new ones, a place that is comfortable for talking, cuddling and kissing. Obviously, you need not limit yourself to the confines of the bedroom this time. The bedroom, in fact, may be the least desirable location. Consider a place that doesn't feel like a classroom, but where you can really get into talking and caressing and kissing—a place that will gently arouse you sexually without putting on any pressure. The living-room couch, a drive-in movie, the back seat of the car, secluded beaches, parks, darkened dance floors and hot tubs are all wonderful places for necking.

Add your personal touches, which may vary considerably depending on where you go. Candlelight, fires, dimmed lights, flowers, music, silence, food and drink are just a few of the possibilities. You might even pull out an old photo album, record album or other carefully stored-away memorabilia that will help set the stage for a little teen-age passion. Use your imagination.

Plan to begin these sessions fully clothed. You might want to wear something special: maybe something particularly flattering, something sexy, or something that brings back happy memories. Take extra time to make yourself exceptionally appealing—but don't feel that once you're dressed you have to stay dressed. As you get wrapped up in your necking, feel free to slowly remove whatever is in the way.

If you haven't kissed romantically for a while, don't push yourselves. Take each step very slowly and allow yourselves to fully enjoy it before taking another. Keep in mind that sexually stimulating kissing is hard for someone who's not ready. Begin with short pecks on the lips that gradually grow into long, slow kisses. As your comfort continues to grow, kiss each other's eyes, ears, neck and shoulders. Experiment to learn how and where you and your lover like to be kissed. If the sexual chemistry begins to really bubble, try using your tongue for French kissing on the mouth and ears.

Use your hands to hug, hold and caress your partner, but at this stage, still avoid touching the genitals or breasts. You may want to hug each other or to hold each other's hands, neck or face while kissing. Or you may find caressing each other's face, arms and legs particularly pleasing.

Focus on enjoying the pleasures of the moment. Make sure you acknowledge both discomfort and pleasure, and be honest with yourself and your partner. As soon as you feel the least bit uneasy, acknowledge the discomfort and suggest a solution. For this assignment, continue to include in your definition of discomfort sexual excitement that begins to force you to want orgasm. If your sexual urge gets that strong, acknowledge it immediately and suggest a way of reducing it. Slowing down a little bit or doing something totally different are two possible solutions. On the other hand, whenever things feel good, make sure your lover knows. Words won't always be necessary since your actions may clearly show the pleasure you're feeling. However, there is nothing wrong and probably lots of good in whispering sweet nothings in your lover's ear.

Relive as much enjoyment of your early courting as you can. As you grow comfortable with necking, think about kissing and caressing anywhere that is sensual (except the breasts and genitals). Be adventurous and playful. No matter what, just make it as much fun as it was years ago.

Schedule three practice sessions to relive the pleasure of necking. When you both are able to easily eliminate discomfort during two consecutive sessions, you are ready to move on to Step 4. If you are enjoying necking so much or simply want to practice more, feel free to schedule as many additional sessions as you would like. However, if at any time after the three sessions you find that you aren't progressing as quickly as you would like, read Alternative 1. Regardless of how things are going, don't forget to reward yourselves after every five sessions.

Here's the list again of possible types of discomfort. Signal discomfort if either of you feels:

- Anxious, nervous, afraid, up tight, edgy or angry;
- Too hot, too cold or aware of any other form of physical discomfort;
- Guilty, ashamed or disgusted;
- Rushed or pressured;
- Compelled to attempt something not prescribed or not wanting to attempt something that had been prescribed;
- That your body was responding unpleasantly or not at all.

ALTERNATIVE 1

Since you are reading this section, you must have had trouble necking. That's too bad, because necking can be a lot of fun. But don't be discouraged, it will be.

Once again, your goal is to enjoy necking. Since you encountered difficulties, you may not be signaling discomfort soon enough. Learning to quickly acknowledge discomfort and then propose a solution should help things get better.

Begin the practice sessions as before. Select a place, create a romantic mood, get yourself ready and be there on time. Begin slowly by doing some hugging, hand-holding and caressing. After a few minutes, try to engage in whatever produces the discomfort. Actually give each other instructions to help bring on the discomfort. Since you are creating this situation, you will be able to identify the discomfort as soon as it begins and signal your partner immediately.

When you signal discomfort, give your partner specific *positive* instructions such as "Kiss me here instead." Avoid negative statements such as "You're doing the wrong thing." If you don't know why you became uncomfortable, return to hugging, hand-holding and caressing. When the discomfort fades, try again to get uncomfortable and then to eliminate the discomfort. Continue this until you feel that you can signal discomfort immediately and then can get comfortable again, or until you realize that continuing this exercise is fruitless.

Do this special assignment for at least three sessions. If you are successful, enjoy necking as long as you both want. On the other hand, if you're not getting anywhere, move on to Alternative 2.

ALTERNATIVE 2

Apparently, some part of necking is causing you quite a bit of discomfort. It is important to get this discomfort under control and replace it with comfort. A good way to do this is by using your imagination. If you can become comfortable imagining an activity, you can learn to enjoy it in reality. In fact, the more pleasurable it is in your imagination, the more pleasurable it will be in real life.

Take a break from your joint sessions. Instead, each of you give yourself four *individual* ten-minute sessions over the next few days to practice using your imagination to create and eliminate discomfort. Success here should help you reach success when you get back to your sessions together.

Find a comfortable chair where you can lean back and relax. Close your eyes, take a few deep breaths and feel your body slowing down. When you feel relatively peaceful, imagine a very pleasant scene such as being praised for work well done, reading in the sunshine or engaging in a favorite sport—whatever. Try to picture the scene as completely as possible and to enjoy the emotional associations. If you really stretch your imagination, it should be almost as good as being there.

When you are able to vividly imagine yourself in this pleasant scene for a minute, stop the scene and imagine yourself necking with your lover. Try to feel all of the emotions; enjoy the pleasure and acknowledge the discomfort. Actually try to experience the discomfort that arises in the practice situation. As soon as you begin to feel it, stop imagining the practice scene and recreate the pleasant scene until the discomfort goes away. Continue this process for the ten-minute session. Each time you imagine yourself necking, try to feel a little more pleasure than the previous time. Little by little you will find yourself working through the discomfort and creating the pleasure you want.

After at least two days and at least four imagery sessions, schedule three necking sessions. If you become uncomfortable during a session, signal your partner and suggest a solution. To help reduce your discomfort, recall the pleasant scene in your imagination. As soon as you are comfortable again, continue the session. Whenever discomfort returns, create the pleasant imagery. If you are successful in eliminating all discomfort during two consecutive sessions, go to Step 4. However, if you are still struggling with discomfort, read Alternative 3.

ALTERNATIVE 3

You apparently are continuing to experience some discomfort while necking. To help you overcome this difficulty, your assignment will be slightly changed.

Begin your practice sessions as usual by getting yourselves comfortable with hugging and holding hands. When you both feel relatively relaxed let the person who is having more difficulty with this assignment act as the leader. For the first half of the session, this person will control the activity. The leader should do most of the kissing and caressing and also make suggestions as to how and where the other partner should kiss and caress. If either partner feels discomfort, it should be acknowledged immediately and eliminated.

At the end of fifteen minutes, the partners should change roles, so that the one who was the leader is now the follower and vice versa. After the thirty-minute period is over, continue kissing and stroking as long as you both are comfortable, changing roles as often as you wish.

Have at least two of these special sessions. When you both feel ready, schedule three regular necking sessions. If you are both able to neck freely without discomfort during two consecutive sessions, begin reading the next assignment. If your difficulties continue, read Alternative 4.

ALTERNATIVE 4

It is important that the two of you be able to complete these sessions comfortably before going on to the next assignment. Discuss your problems, being open and frank with each other regarding your comfort and discomfort. This will help you eliminate your discomfort more quickly and build the pleasure you both desire.

Success will come with perseverance. You seem to need more homework at this stage. You can get it by starting this chapter over again as if it were the first time. As you continue to practice, use the insight you have acquired to increase your pleasure and decrease your discomfort. Schedule and hold sessions frequently, and make certain that you signal discomfort immediately. Don't worry about not progressing quickly. Comfort comes with time and practice.

Continue to reward yourselves after every five sessions. This will help you provide support for each other and encourage you to overcome any difficulties you are still experiencing. If you feel professional counseling would make things easier, consider talking to a counselor.

CHAPTER 10

Step 4: Show and Tell

RULES, rules, rules. No matter where we look we find rules about sex. Although not always well defined or even acknowledged openly, these rules influence all of us from the day we are born until the day we die. Although most of them control what we should not do, others control not only what we should do, but also when, where, how much, and how well. The firmness of these rules varies from generation to generation, but their basic themes remain relatively constant. Their existence undeniably benefits society in developing responsible sexual behavior in children and adults. On the other hand, when adults unquestioningly accept too many rules about sex, they may pay the price of inhibited pleasure and affection.

While sexual responsibility grows in part out of

society's restrictions, true sexual intimacy grows out of the freedom to be oneself. In the case of sex, freedom is the ability to openly show and genuinely enjoy physical and emotional pleasure. Being free to indulge in the pleasures of one's desires leads to becoming emotionally close, loving openly and soaring sexually. Memorable sex stems from the freedom to enjoy unrestricted emotional and physical heights. Neither inhibitions nor fears of failure get in the way. Ecstasy grows as romantic thoughts and indescribable physical pleasure replace seriousness and the distractions of day-to-day concerns. Sexual pleasure can frequently rise to such a peak that it fills your days with joy.

All of us are born with the ability to soar sexually, but unfortunately, many of us have unconsciously learned to restrict this ability. Fortunately, it can often be easily set free by thoughtfully questioning the rules we've been following. Discarding unnecessary rules and revising overly strict ones can bring a wonderful freedom. As the influence of unessential rules fades, new sexual heights quickly come into view.

The sexual revolution and widespread sexual freedom during the 1960s and '70s severely challenged innumerable long-standing sexual rules. At times, it seemed as if all the old sexual rules had been tossed aside. Hedonism seemed to sweep through our society and often replaced traditional family-oriented attitudes. Sexual freedom and indulgence seemed to be the norm rather than the exception. As the sexual revolution ran its course, though, it became obvious that the old rules had not vanished, but were instead being observed selectively. Rules for the development of responsible behavior and, especially, rules for the control of child and adult sexual abuse not only remained but were toughened. On the other hand, rules restricting sexual pleasure between consenting adults relaxed and stayed relaxed.

Sexual rules for and about children will always be necessary because they provide a way for society to attempt to insure orderly growth for every child. Well-defined rules protect children until they are mature enough to make good decisions for themselves and at the same time discourage adults from making poor decisions regarding children. Rules for children are particularly necessary for controlling incest, abuse, unwanted pregnancy, and disease while children are growing to maturity.

The age-old sexual rules for children still tend to discourage "premature" sexual activity. Almost from the day they are born, children are taught to suppress any behavior that appears sexual. As they gradually mature into adults, they are permitted more and more sexual activity, but limits still remain. Most of today's adults have grown up with traditional sexual rules. As children, today's adults encountered, in varying degrees of intensity, many of the following restrictions: Whenever babies touched their genitals, their parents pulled their hands away; young children were told not to play doctor and cautioned not to touch their private parts; adolescents were told not to masturbate and sometimes warned that masturbation could result in hairy palms, blindness, deafness, or even craziness; teen-agers were prohibited from dating until they were "old enough" and discouraged from sexual relations prior to marriage.

When adulthood was finally reached, people found (and still find) themselves accepting new freedoms, selecting new ways of fulfilling their desires, needs and whims. Adulthood is a time when people should take responsibility for their own lives. Instead of continuing to accept and blindly follow the rules of our youth, each of us can choose the rules by which we intend to live. As most people learn, rules about sex change dramatically between childhood and adulthood. In fact, many of the activities that were previously taboo become not only acceptable, but encouraged. Rising to meet this challenge of adult freedom is necessary for true sexual pleasure.

Despite the help offered by parents, friends and teachers to develop beneficial adult sexual attitudes, almost everyone has trouble shedding at least some of the beliefs imposed upon them as children and adolescents. When change does take place, all too often it's accompanied by guilt, fear or other emotional or even physical discomfort. Many people shed their childhood restrictions by going through a period of rebellion during which they appear to toss aside all sexual rules, after which they gradually return to more traditional lives. At the other extreme, some have difficulty changing even a little. For them, the old sexual rules and the expected punishment for breaking them remain a solid part of their lives. Most of us wind up somewhere in between, going through some rebellion and maintaining some of the old rules.

The inability to discard unnecessary childhood restraints seriously interferes with adult relationships, often inhibiting the ability to be close to someone else and to enjoy the pleasures of intimacy. Instead of allowing themselves to freely enjoy sexual intercourse, people who suffer these restraints restrict both their feelings and their actions. The quality of their intimacy and their relationships can never reach their full potential.

Think about the common rules that you and your spouse learned when you were younger. Since society tends to make very different and often conflicting sets of rules for girls and boys, you will probably find that you each learned some very similar and some very different *do*'s and *don't*'s. You will most likely see that these differing standards caused different types of problems, and you may even find that leftover conflicting expectations have put noticeable stress on your sexual as well as your whole marital relationship.

Traditionally, most girls were taught that *no one*, even themselves, should be allowed to touch their private parts. As they became adolescents, they were warned that masturbation is wrong and even dirty. When they were allowed to date, they were told that sex is only for marriage. Only bad girls, it is still sometimes suggested, are intimate before marriage. As a girl reached adulthood, this rule might have changed to allow sex before marriage, but "only if things are serious." As a result, sex became basically connected to love. A young woman often concluded that sex was necessary to keep a man around but simultaneously learned that men don't want to marry women who had been too sexually active.

As girls grew up, they learned to expect men to be the initiators and aggressors. Further, they learned to be wary of a man's advances, to keep control of a sexual situation, and to make sure his intentions were honorable. Consequently, at a time when all adolescents have an enormous sex drive, young women learned to hold back their true sexual feelings. As adults, men can have sex just for fun, but for the women who grew up with these rules, sex often needs to be serious.

Little boys were usually taught that, except for urinating, touching their genitals was wrong, but in contrast to girls, they soon learned to ignore this rule. Since time immemorial, as boys reach adolescence, it has been generally accepted that they will tell dirty jokes with their peers and masturbate. In his relationships with women, a young man quickly learned that he was expected to be the sexual aggressor and the sexually knowledgeable partner. The result is that many men believe that their male self-esteem is measured by their sexual success. Some men value sex primarily as fun and games, and continue to seek the satisfaction of pursuit and conquest. Despite their apparent freedom, these men often suffer the pressure to always function perfectly and the inability to enjoy the tenderness of sex.

As you became a man or woman, you selected whom you wanted to date and with whom to become intimate. You also decided when and to what extent to become intimate. You may have decided that sex without love or marriage was fine. But just because you were old enough to make your own decisions didn't mean that the lessons you'd learned and attitudes you'd developed as a child were erased. Instead you may have experienced internal conflicts about what you really believed as well as conflicts in adjusting to the expectations and desires of your partner.

Such conflicts are not limited to one-night stands, casual relationships or flings. Men and women frequently carry their childhood attitudes into caring and loving relationships. In fact, almost all married couples experience sexual difficulties at one time or another. They find, instead of open and satisfying love-making, emotional boundaries and restraints on their sexual satisfaction.

Now is the time for you get rid of any inhibitions that stand in the way of your sexual pleasure. This may mean that a woman needs to learn to be able to accept and enjoy the physical pleasure of sex, while a man needs to be able to enjoy the feelings of sex without the pressure to perform. Your own experience may be totally different, but in any case, you will now be encouraged to break some of the old rules. In fact, you will not only be encouraged to break some of the rules, but to enjoy breaking them.

Your next assignment is to do something that you were probably forbidden to do as a child: play doctor. That's right, it's show-and-tell time. For three practice sessions, you will simply take a good look at your own body and look at, touch and kiss your partner's body. If this seems old hat, you may be surprised to find it more useful than you think. You might very well learn something new about each of your bodies, or you might encounter some discomfort that you didn't know you had. You are to make sure that you are *comfortable* with your own body and your partner's. Try any activities that intellectually you know are OK, but that you have not accepted emotionally as OK for you. Just keep in mind that *comfort* is your goal, not excitement.

Be optimistic. Prepare yourself mentally to believe that breaking needless old rules is all right. At times, it may seem difficult or painful, but do your best to stretch your level of comfort. Try activities that you have not tried before, as well as things that have made you uncomfortable in the past. Start with the conviction that you are going to enjoy what you do and then make your beliefs come true.

You will probably find your bedroom as good a place as any for this assignment. Since your goal is simply comfort and not arousal, you just need a place where you can have privacy and feel relaxed. If you want to have a practice session in a hot tub, a secluded cabin or a tent in the woods, that's fine, too.

You could begin undressed or start out clothed and undress during the session. When you both feel ready, start by caressing and kissing each other. Get involved in any of the activities you've enjoyed in the past, but for these first few minutes, avoid any genital contact. When you both are ready, begin playing doctor.

Imagine that the two of you have never been

sexually intimate before. Imagine that you have never seen or touched your own or your lover's genitals. Think of yourselves as students learning about the structure, texture and functioning of each of your bodies, without being concerned about sexual arousal. Together explore one partner's body and then the other's. Throughout the exploration, just make sure that you both remain comfortable, whether you're looking at and touching your lover's body or your own. If you feel any discomfort, acknowledge it immediately and resolve it. If you find anything particularly pleasing or have anything interesting to share about your body, let it be known.

Begin as if it were actually show-and-tell. Together, visually explore one partner's body and then the other's. Take a good look, all over. Pay particular attention to the breasts, buttocks and genitals. The person being viewed should act as the leader. Any areas that have particularly sensitive reactions, either pleasant or unpleasant, should be pointed out. Especially when viewing the genitals, the leader should describe sensations and functioning. Lift and move around to get a better look. Get comfortable both looking at your partner's sexual areas and at having your partner look at yours.

As you become comfortable looking, begin to explore each other's body with your hands. Glide your hands over your spouse's body and move your spouse's hands over yours. Notice the differences in texture and depth of skin. Gently touch those areas that frequently feel extremely sensual or sexual such as the ears, lips, eyelids, back of the neck, inner thighs, back of the knees and ankles. Take note of the touches that feel especially pleasurable.

Closely examine one partner's breasts, buttocks and genitals. Get comfortable with having your own sexual areas touched and with touching the sexual areas of your spouse. Discover where and how each of you likes to be touched. Watch how each body responds when touched. See if muscles pull tight, muscles loosen, skin responds or lubrication starts. Of utmost importance, watch how the other partner responds emotionally.

As you grow comfortable with the touching of both your bodies, begin to kiss your lover's entire body. Start with kissing each other on the lips. If you aren't already doing it, try French kissing. Eventually kiss anywhere that you both agree may be sensual or sexual. Again try the ears, eyelids, back of the neck, back of the knees, ankles and breasts.

If you both desire it, try kissing each other's genitals. Be open-minded, but don't do anything that offends you. As with all sexual activities, oral sex needs to be voluntary and is not a necessity. Many people greatly enjoy oral sex, and some enjoy it so much that they find it easier to reach orgasm through oral sex than intercourse. Others, however, find it totally unacceptable. Since it is often a topic for disagreement, each of you should at least express your views. If either one of you does not want to do it, don't try it now. But don't be surprised if you change your mind in the future.

Don't get too serious during the practice sessions. In fact, do just the opposite. Instead of just touching your partner, you might want to spend an afternoon body-painting and then have the fun of scrubbing it off in a shared shower. Instead of just kissing your partner, try some jam or whipped cream. Spoon or spray it on and then enjoy together the pleasure of licking it off.

No matter what you try, focus on increasing your comfort while looking at and touching your own body, and looking at, touching and kissing your partner's body. Keep in mind that sexual arousal now is nice, but is *not* your goal. If you should find a touch particularly arousing, don't restrict it unless you are nearing the point where orgasm is unavoidable. If you do get this excited, acknowledge it as discomfort and reduce the excitement to avoid orgasm during the session. You can feel free to stimulate yourself to orgasm after the session is over.

It is likely that you will now encounter more pleasure and also more fears than in earlier sessions. Make sure you let your lover know how you are feeling. While "ooh's," "ah's," moans and groans clearly express your pleasure, don't forget to use words too. As for fears, these are often the most difficult discomforts for which to suggest a solution. Often, the best thing to do is to acknowledge the fear and slowly try to go on with the assignment. Just the open recognition and acknowledgment of fear can make you feel better. Besides, once you've managed to describe the fear, your partner can act appropriately to minimize your discomfort. Your partner can give you reassurance and avoid doing whatever it is that makes you uncomfortable.

You may be surprised at how much you can share now with your partner. Sharing your physical feelings through communication, both physical and verbal, is the key to this assignment. By hearing yourself acknowledge both pleasure and discomfort to your partner, you will be more in touch with your body and the sensations it likes. This will help you feel more positive about pleasure you can share, and about your increased control over it. Your positive acknowledgment will also make your partner feel good about helping to create some of this pleasure.

Schedule three thirty-minute practice sessions. If you both desire, feel free to lengthen any of them. When you both are able to eliminate discomfort during two consecutive sessions, you are ready to move on to Step 5. If you want more time to practice, schedule as many additional sessions as you both want. However, if at any time after the three sessions, you find you aren't progressing as quickly as you would like, read Alternative 1.

Remember that discomfort is any feeling of uneasiness. Here again is the list of things you need to be aware of. Signal discomfort, if either of you feel:

- Anxious, nervous, afraid, up tight, edgy or angry;
- Too hot, too cold or aware of any other form of physical discomfort;
- Guilty, ashamed or disgusted;

- Rushed or pressured;
- Compelled to attempt an activity not pre-scribed (such as intercourse or reaching or-gasm) or not wanting to attempt an activity that had been prescribed;
- That your body was responding unpleasantly or not at all.

Regardless of how well things are going, don't forget to reward yourselves. If the wife has decided to do the special exercises described on pages 85 to 87, she should keep on doing them.

ALTERNATIVE 1

You're having trouble playing doctor. That's too bad, but you will learn to enjoy it with a little more practice. It's an important step in your progress to-wards satisfying sex, so take as much time as you need to get comfortable with it.

Your goal is still to play doctor. Since you are able to massage each other comfortably but not play doctor, you may simply not be signaling discomfort soon enough in this assignment. Learning to acknowledge discomfort quickly and then proposing a solution should help you succeed.

Begin the practice sessions as before. Select a lo-cation, get yourself ready and be there on time. Begin slowly with some small talk, hugging, hand-holding and caressing. After a few minutes, try to engage in the activites that produced discomfort—in fact, actually give each other instructions to bring on the discomfort. Since you are creating this situation, you will be able to identify the discomfort as soon as it begins and signal your lover immediately.

When you signal discomfort, gently give your partner specific *positive* corrective instructions such as "Touch me there more softly," or "I'd rather not be touched there—touch me here." Avoid any blaming or negative statements such as "You're doing it all wrong." If you don't know why you become uncomfortable, return to hugging, hand-holding and caressing. When the discomfort fades, try again to get uncomfortable, eliminate the discomfort immediately and get comfortable again, or stop if you realize that continuing this exercise is fruitless.

Do this special assignment for at least three sessions. If you are successful, enjoy playing doctor as long as you both want. On the other hand, if the discomfort continues, move on to Alternative 2.

ALTERNATIVE 2

Apparently, some part of playing doctor is causing you quite a bit of discomfort. It is important to get this discomfort under control and replace it with comfort. A good way to do this is by using your imagination. If you can become comfortable imagining an

activity, you can learn to enjoy it in reality. In fact, the
better it is in your imagination, the better it will be in
real life.

Take a break from your practice sessions together. Instead, each of you should have four individual ten-minute sessions over the next few days.
During these sessions, you will each individually practice using your imagination to create and eliminate
discomfort. Success here should help you be successful when you resume the practice sessions
together.

Find a comfortable chair where you can lean back
and relax. Close your eyes, take a few deep breaths,
and feel your body slowing down. When you feel relatively peaceful, imagine a very pleasant scene such as
lying in the sun on a beach after swimming, nuzzling
a puppy, or whatever you particularly enjoy. Try to
picture this scene as completely as possible and enjoy
all the emotions associated with it. Stretch your imagination so you can almost feel that you're there.

When you're able to vividly picture yourself in
this pleasant scene for a whole minute, end the scene
and imagine yourself playing doctor with your lover.
Try to feel all the emotions you felt in the sessions—
enjoy the pleasure and recall the discomfort. Try to
actually experience the discomfort that arises in the
practice situation. As soon as you begin to feel it, stop
the practice scene and go back to the pleasant scene
until the discomfort goes away.

Continue this process for the duration of the ten-
minute session. Each time you imagine yourself
playing doctor, try to feel a little more pleasure than

the previous time. Little by little you will find yourself working through the discomfort and creating the pleasure you are seeking.

After two days, and at least four imagery sessions, schedule three sessions for playing doctor. If you become uncomfortable during a session, signal your partner and suggest a solution. To help you reduce your discomfort, bring back the pleasant scene in your imagination. As soon as you feel comfortable again, continue the session. Whenever discomfort returns, create the pleasant imagery.

If you are successful in eliminating discomfort during two consecutive sessions, skip to Step 5. However, if you are still struggling with the discomfort, read Alternative 3.

ALTERNATIVE 3

It's important that the two of you be able to complete the playing-doctor activities comfortably before advancing to the next assignment. Discuss the problems you're having and be open and frank with each other regarding comfort and discomfort. This will help you get rid of your discomfort more quickly and build the pleasure you're looking for. If you find the discussion troublesome or unrewarding, you might want to discuss your discomfort with a professional counselor.

Be persistent, and success will come. You seem to to need more practice at this stage, so start this assignment over again as if it were the first time. As you learn to increase your pleasure and decrease your discomfort, you will feel and see your progress. Schedule practice sessions frequently. Make sure that you signal discomfort immediately, and don't worry about not progressing quickly. Comfort comes with time and practice. Some couples find assignments easy that others find difficult, and there are no rules as to who'll slow down where.

Continue to reward yourselves after every five sessions that you complete. By now you must have enjoyed some good rewards and can see how the rewards give you support and help overcome any difficulties.

CHAPTER 11

Step 5: Learning the Territory

SEX is love. Sex is tenderness. Sex is caring. Sex is also intense passion and enormous physical pleasure. It's thunder and lightning in the bedroom. Satisfying sex is feeling so good all over that it shows.

Despite our capacity for sexual ecstasy, millions of us go through life exploring very little of our sexual potential. The territory between our waistline and knees remains relatively uncharted. Dissatisfied though we may be with our sex lives, we usually do little if anything about it; we waste one of life's greatest pleasures because we don't know how to go about fulfilling our own sexual potential.

To fully enjoy sex, we have to know the territory. We need to understand what turns us on and what doesn't, where we like to be touched and how. True, we can learn a lot from books, but there's nothing like hands-on experience. Books can tell us what most people like, but only we know what *we* ourselves like.

Taking the time to find out what turns you on is essential. Recognizing your own sexual tastes will give you invaluable control over your own sexuality and the satisfaction you get from it. Although you may never have realized that you had this ability to control your sexual feelings, you do have it—and developing it is a must for sexual satisfaction. By knowing what stimulates you, you can control your level of sexual arousal and the speed and level of your excitement. You can decide whether to remain pleasantly aroused or to seek new heights. You can train your body to function any way you want. You will be able to have greater arousal and more exciting orgasms than you've ever had before. And, as your physical pleasure grows, your emotional pleasure will flourish. You'll desire sex more, enjoy sex more and be a better sexual partner. Both you and your spouse will be amazed by the dramatic changes in your sexual happiness.

Sharing these new discoveries with each other will open up a more exciting and joyous marriage. You will feel more sexually fulfilled and your partner will cherish the satisfaction of providing you with so much pleasure. However (as always), you can't expect your lover to read your mind. You must explain what pleases you.

Back to the basics. To develop the necessary understanding of your sexuality, you need first to study how *your* body functions. You need to stimulate your body and see how you respond, to investigate what *you* like and what *you* dislike. The more curious you are, the more you will learn. You will find out what kinds of stimulation, techniques and foreplay drive you to unlimited sexual heights.

Although you may be tempted to do this research with your partner, you will each learn more if you start the research with your own body. Nobody can react to or identify your feelings faster than you can. If you like a particular caress, you can continue it and perhaps make it even more enjoyable. On the other hand, if you find a particular caress annoying, you can stop it immediately. You can learn what feels best for you.

By stimulating yourself you can teach your body to respond the way you want it to. You can teach it to get excited more quickly or slowly; you can make these responses almost automatic so that your body will respond as you would like it to in any sexual situation. With your senses heightened, your body will become more interested in sexual gratification, and sexual arousal will be easier. Orgasm will occur more easily, more intensely and, most important, whenever you want it.

Teaching your body to respond the way you want it to may sound strange at first, but when you think about it, this is something you've been doing all your life in nonsexual areas. When you first started driving a car you had to think about every motion. As you became more experienced, you thought about the motions less and less until gradually they became second nature. It's the same with sex. When you're not used to getting excited or having orgasms, your body doesn't know how to act. But once it's learned to respond as you want it to, the natural responses come easier and easier—like second nature.

You may be thinking now that this all sounds very unromantic and mechanical. It's not. In fact, it's just the opposite. Teaching your body to respond the way you want leads to better sex, which leads to more and better passion, which leads to a more trusting and loving marriage. If your body were a sports car, how much fun could you have if you didn't know how to get out of first gear? You might have the pride of possessing it, but your relationship to it would be far from genuinely satisfying. With love-making and marriage, as with driving, you need to learn the basics before you can learn the extra skills.

Despite knowing about the benefits of understanding your sexual functioning, you may still have reservations about stimulating yourself. You may be concerned that some of the old wives' tales are true or that only deviants do it. You may still be carrying some of the inhibitions imposed on you in your childhood. The fact is, many married people enjoy self-stimulation. They find that besides relieving sexual pressures it simply feels good. Not only that, but they don't go crazy, go blind, or find hair growing on the palms of their hands. Many do have one thing in common: they enjoy sex. Not only do they enjoy the pleasures of self-stimulation, they also enjoy their sexual relations with their lovers.

SELF-DISCOVERY

Touching their own genitals is natural for men,

since urinating requires a man to hold his penis. Self-stimulation is also natural for most men and at one time or another, most have done it. In contrast, a great number of women have never touched themselves or looked at their genitals. This doesn't mean that it's bad for women, it just means that they haven't done it.

For some of you, self-stimulation may be a totally new experience. You may even have fears that have prevented you from trying it. *These fears are not unusual.* At this point, it is important for you to decide, at least intellectually if not emotionally, that self-stimulation is OK. As you progress through this assignment, you will see that self-stimulation is not bad for you, that you're actually going to benefit from it, and that you even have the right to enjoy it. If you are having trouble accepting the idea, simply think of it as one step toward your ultimate goal of great sex. Once you have made the decision that self-stimulation is OK for you, you are more than halfway there.

As always, what you're after during the sessions is to remain comfortable. Although you will be seeking arousal, continue to focus on recognizing and getting rid of discomfort. Once you learn to maintain comfort, sexual arousal and orgasm will follow.

To prepare for your self-stimulation, schedule three practice sessions with your partner. Begin each session together by relaxing and enjoying carefree kissing. Be teen-agers on a date again, then move on to the adult pleasures of both sensual and sexual touching. When you're both ready, one of you will go into another room. Agree on how long you'll be apart, allowing at least fifteen minutes for your investigations. When the time is up, get back together and continue cuddling and petting.

Decide on how much time you each want for your personal investigation and make sure it's enough. You won't want to feel rushed or pressured, especially if self-stimulation is new to you, so although we've suggested fifteen minutes, you may want to give yourself a lot more time than that. Take it slow and easy. In any case, women should expect to take a little longer than men. In fact, women should not be surprised if it takes quite a while before the excitement starts to grow. But keep in mind that *this is not a competition.* It is simply a time for each of you to learn more about your own body. If, on the other hand, you should find that you have left-over time while waiting for your partner, enjoy a little rest with your pleasant memories.

Being alone will help reduce any initial self-consciousness, particularly if self-stimulation is new to you. Learning to feel comfortable as your arousal grows may be much easier alone than with your partner, especially when you begin to do things that may surprise you such as squirming, moaning or yelling. But don't let these stop you from enjoying the pleasure. Everyone does at least some of them.

Choose a place where you can be relaxed and comfortable. A bedroom is the most obvious place and as good as any. Since you certainly don't want to be disturbed, lock the door, disconnect the phone and make arrangements so the kids can't disturb you. Add a little atmosphere if it will help you get relaxed and in the mood. Do whatever it takes. You may want to put fresh sheets on the bed beforehand, turn down the lights, put on some music and have a drink. A relaxing candle-lit bubble bath might be the way to begin.

Start your discovery by lying down. Close your eyes and allow yourself to relax, then take several long deep breaths to relax further. As you grow relaxed, move into a seated or semi-seated position, maybe leaning against several pillows pushed against the head of your bed. When you're comfortable, close your eyes again and begin to touch every part of your body from your head to your feet. As you touch each part, pay attention to the feel of your bone structure, to the feel of your skin and to your body's reaction to your touching. After you have felt your entire body, massage some of the more sensitive areas. Try to find those hidden sensitive areas such as the bottoms of your feet, your ankles, the backs of your knees, under your arms or the back of your neck. Try different pressures, movements and speeds. As you find an area that responds to the massage, try to find the most enjoyable type of touching. Just try to enjoy the self-caressing. Use massage oil or lotion if it helps to reduce friction. Continue massaging as long as you remain comfortable.

At first you may get little or no enjoyment. But, as you continue your sessions alone you will increasingly enjoy the massage, relaxation, excitement and, finally, orgasm. When you're comfortable with caressing your own body, begin to stroke your breasts and genitals. Don't be concerned with stimulation. Just try to learn where you enjoy being touched and how. As you discover the areas that respond positively, concentrate on them. Do whatever is comfortable and try to avoid discomfort. Just enjoy the pleasure you're experiencing at the moment, and don't be concerned about pleasure you have not yet felt.

Let your sexual fantasies roam freely. Fantasies are normal and powerful. Simply thinking about romantic or sexy scenes can easily arouse most people. Encourage your fantasies. Read a steamy passage from an erotic book, look at some titillating pictures or just think about somebody you find really sexy. Using erotic aids like these can definitely be exciting and they certainly are no sign of weakness, perversion or disloyalty to your spouse.

If you have never stimulated yourself before, the following should be helpful.

For a man: Put some warmed massage oil on your hands and begin to rub your entire genital area. Rubbing almost any part of your genitals should provide an enjoyable sensation, with some parts providing far more stimulation than others. Lift your penis and notice a ridge running the length of it. This is often the center of excitement. Begin by rubbing this ridge lightly. By rubbing it just slightly below the head of your penis, you should find an extremely sensitive spot that produces a particularly nice sensation. Rubbing this spot by making soft, slow circular movements with the fingers should make the feeling get better and better. As you continue to rub, your penis will grow in size. As it enlarges, begin to make your circles larger. Stroke the entire ridge lightly as your penis becomes fully erect and continue to add pressure as it stiffens. Encircle your penis with your hand so that your fingers are on the ridge and your thumb is on the other side of your penis. Begin full pump-like strokes with your hand around your penis. Gradually tightening your fingers and increasing the speed of your strokes should create more and more sensation.

For a woman: Begin by rubbing your entire genital area. You might also find some baby or massage oil useful if you are not producing enough natural lubrication. Since your clitoris is the most responsive part of your genitals, you might wish to concentrate your rubbing there. However, don't forget the rest of your body; many women also enjoy alternately caressing their breasts and clitoris. Try massaging at different rates and pressures. As your excitement grows, you will probably want to stroke your clitoral area more and more. Some women prefer massaging the clitoris directly, but many find it too sensitive. Find out what is most enjoyable for you and don't worry if you temporarily lose the excitement. The area of sensation often shifts, and your clitoral area may become numb or tender for a few minutes. If this happens, simply rub along its sides. Once you find an exciting area, keep rubbing it. If it moves, find a new one. By adjusting to your body, you can make the excitement grow and grow.

Both husband and wife should each keep in mind that *you are in control*. You can start and stop whenever you want, and you can massage at whatever rate and pressure you prefer. Find out what you like and then do it. If you become embarrassed about stimulating yourself remember that what you're doing, far from being harmful, is simply a natural enjoyable function—a means of releasing sexual tension and creating pleasure. Discovering your own likes and dislikes is the best way to learn things that you can later share with your lover for better and better sex.

Be inventive. Don't be afraid to move around and try different positions. Sit, stand or lie down on your side, back or stomach. Try rubbing your genitals with both hands. Sometimes you can roll from side to side on a pillow so that your body rubs your genitals. A combination of body weight, hand rubbing and fantasies is often very exciting. Stay in touch with your body and watch the way it reacts. Feel your muscles tense or relax. Notice your breathing. Is it faster or slower? Are you sweating? Perhaps your lips and mouth are dry or your skin feels tight. You may get goose pimples or your toes may curl. Perhaps a woman's breasts may swell and her nipples become erect. Keep doing whatever feels good; stroke wherever and however you want.

As you grow more comfortable with your sessions alone, you will find yourself concentrating more intently on your body's responses and the kinds of touching that give your genitals the most rewarding feelings. Your body will guide you to more and more intense excitement. The trick is to concentrate on what you are feeling at the moment, and *not* to think about what you *hope* to feel or *ought* to feel. Compare it to climbing a flight of stairs; concentrate on each step and don't look up to see how near or far the top is. Watch your body change as your excitement grows. Your muscles will become tense. Your breath will get faster. Your genitals will begin to throb. Your mind will fill with fantasies. If you are approaching orgasm, you may feel like gasping for air. You may want to moan, scream or yell. Your body may toss and turn. Your pelvic muscles will get tighter and tighter and you will have the feeling of pressure and explosion. After orgasm, you will grow peaceful and exhausted.

If you are able to have an orgasm, that's great. If not, don't worry or push yourself. Just enjoy the sexual sensations as they occur. Orgasm will come in time as long as you remain comfortable and concentrate on the sensations of the moment. Reaching orgasm is like falling asleep—you can't force it to happen; you can only let it occur naturally. But the more you self-stimulate, the easier it will be for you to become sexually excited, whether you have orgasm or not. What you're doing now, remember, is training your body to respond through practice. If you become uncomfortable at any time during the investigation, change what you're doing. You may want to stroke your body in places other than your genitals, or just remain lying there.

After you have finished your investigation and your agreed-upon separation time has passed, the two of you should get back together again, feeling free to stroke, massage and touch each other however you want, including breasts and genitals. If you feel like it, share your individual experiences. Otherwise, just enjoy the pleasure of being together. If you have encountered discomfort, after the two of you have come back together tell your partner and see if you can think of a way to eliminate it.

If you'd like more information on stimulating yourself, read *The Sensuous Man* by "M," pages 45-52, or *The Sensuous Woman* by "J," pages 43-52. You might also want to pick up some sexually stimulating magazines—*Playboy* or *Playgirl*—or such books as *Lady Chatterley's Lover, My Secret Garden, Candy* or *The Pearl.* Or you might want to stop in at one of the ever-growing number of "love shops" that specialize in almost any fantasy-pleasers you can think of.

Don't be concerned if your reservations about self-stimulation persist. They will gradually fade as you learn more about your body and as you realize that self-stimulation is normal and has no harmful side effects. You might want to discuss these concerns with your spouse or a close friend. Just acknowledging them often diminishes them, and you may discover that your concerns are not uncommon or, on the other hand, that self-stimulation is more common than you'd thought.

You are now ready to set the stage for your session. You will need two comfortable rooms, two clocks and some warmed lubricant for each of you. Add some juicy sexual fantasies and you are ready to begin. To speed up your progress, feel free to schedule some investigation sessions by yourself. Take the additional private time to slowly research your personal sensations so that you don't feel pressured to rush or to perform.

Schedule your three practice sessions now. If you

are both able to reach satisfying orgasms comfortably during two consecutive sessions, go on to Step 6 to share your discoveries with your partner. If you want more practice sessions, feel free to schedule as many as you like. If, at any time after three sessions, either of you feels that you are not progressing, read Alternative 1.

Remember that discomfort is any feeling of uneasiness. Here's the list of things you need to be aware of during the self-stimulation exercises. Signal discomfort, if either of you feels:

- Anxious, nervous, afraid, up tight, edgy or angry;
- Too hot, too cold or aware of any other form of physical discomfort;
- Guilty, ashamed, or disgusted;
- Rushed or pressured;
- Compelled to attempt an activity not prescribed (such as intercourse or bringing each other to orgasm) or not wanting to attempt an activity that had been prescribed;
- That your body was responding unpleasantly or not at all.

ALTERNATIVE 1

Apparently one or both of you is having difficulty with self-stimulation. This certainly isn't unusual, and it certainly is correctable. Continued practice and eliminating discomfort remain the keys to success.

Most likely, one of you is having more difficulty than the other. The slower partner needs to avoid feeling any guilt for disappointing the faster partner. Usually the faster partner is so pleased about the slower partner even participating that no disappointment exists. Despite this acceptance, the slower partner may still feel some frustation and guilt. To avoid or at least minimize these feelings, stay in touch with the pleasurable sensations that you're having, however few they may be. Try not to be concerned about pleasures you have not yet gotten to. They will come in time.

Schedule three sessions for the two of you as a couple as before. The partner who has not yet reached orgasm might also want to schedule several individual sessions for additional practice. Before each session together, you may each want to do some preparation. First, you might warm some lubricant and put some in a separate container for each of you. Second, you may want to spend more time to get yourself into the mood. Of utmost importance, make sure that you are there and ready at the designated time.

Begin the session together by enjoying any of the activities of the previous steps. When both of you are comfortable, separate into different rooms and remember to each take a container of oil. While separate, begin to stroke and massage yourselves. As you grow more and more comfortable, begin to stroke your genitals for as long as possible while remaining comfortable. Use the oil as often as you want. If orgasm happens comfortably, let it come, but don't make yourself uncomfortable in an attempt to have an orgasm. With sustained comfort, orgasm will happen involuntarily.

If either of you experiences discomfort with self-stimulation, practice the following self-awareness exercises. Apply the warm lubricant to your genitals. Begin caressing yourself in the area close to your genitals and, if you like, your breasts. Gradually massage closer and closer to your genital areas with your hands. If you're uncomfortable at any time, stop right away and return to caresses that do feel comfortable. Then start again, but more slowly, toward whatever made you uncomfortable. When the discomfort occurs, return once more to caresses that feel comfortable. Keep repeating these exercises to reduce and eventually get rid of your discomfort.

When you have succeeded in eliminating discomfort, continue to massage your genitals. Explore and caress your genitals and the areas around them. Focus on the differences in sensations. If you feel discomfort again, keep practicing these self-awareness exercises. If you still have difficulty, do whatever it takes to get rid of the discomfort. Rejoin your lover at the agreed-upon time and participate in any of the massaging, caressing and kissing of the previous steps.

Remember to give yourselves a reward after every five practice sessions. As soon as you are both able to comfortably reach orgasm during two consecutive self-stimulation sessions, progress to the Step 6.

If you are unsuccessful after three sessions, read Alternative 2.

ALTERNATIVE 2

Using your imagination is a great way to overcome discomfort. If you can become comfortable with an activity in your imagination, you can often learn to enjoy the same comfort in reality. Usually, in fact, the more enjoyable something is in your imagination, the more enjoyable it will be in real life.

Take a break from your joint practice sessions. Instead, the one (or two) of you who is having difficulty with self-stimulation should have four individual ten-minute sessions over the next few days. During these sessions, use your imagination to practice creating and getting rid of discomfort. Success here should help you reach success in your practice sessions together.

Find a comfortable chair you can lean back and relax in. Close your eyes, take a few deep breaths, and feel your body slowing down. When you feel relatively peaceful, imagine a very pleasant scene such as lying on a beach after swimming, feeling the warmth of the sun or doing something you especially like. Try to picture this scene as completely as possible along with the emotions that go with it. Really stretch your imagination so it will be almost as good as being there.

When you are able to vividly imagine yourself in this pleasant scene for a minute, stop the scene and imagine yourself peacefully lying in bed. Picture yourself beginning to massage your body, but not your genitals. When you can comfortably visualize this scene, then begin to imagine that you are stimulating your genitals. Try to feel all the emotions, enjoying the pleasure and acknowledging the discomfort. Actually try to experience the discomfort that arises during the practice sessions. As soon as you begin to feel the discomfort, turn off this scene and recreate the pleasant scene until the discomfort has completely gone. Continue this process for the ten-minute session. Each time you imagine stimulating yourself, try to feel a little more of the pleasure than the previous time. Little by little you will find yourself working through the discomfort and creating the pleasure you're seeking. When you feel comfortable imagining self-stimulation, try to imagine yourself actually reaching orgasm. Try to see and feel the changes in your body. If fantasizing orgasm causes you discomfort, use the same process to get comfortable with orgasm.

After two days and at least four imagination sessions, schedule three self-stimulation sessions. If you are the only one having difficulty, you may want to have most of these by yourself. If you become uncomfortable during a session, use your imagination to help you reduce the discomfort. Quietly lie there and imagine the pleasant scene. As soon as you are comfortable again, continue the session. Whenever discomfort returns, go back to the pleasant imagery.

If you are both successful in reaching orgasm during two consecutive self-stimulation practice sessions, skip to Step 6. If you are still having difficulty reaching orgasm, read Alternative 3 and remember to continue rewarding yourselves.

ALTERNATIVE 3

People are often unable to reach orgasm simply because they haven't stimulated their genitals long enough. Although they may think that it should not take so long, they need to realize that it may take longer because it is new to them. While people who are accustomed to stimulating their own genitals may require only a couple of minutes to reach orgasm, those who are new to this activity may take at least a half hour.

For this assignment, your goal will be to comfortably stimulate your own genitals for thirty minutes. As you maintain comfort for prolonged periods of time, sexual excitement will grow and orgasm will follow. If orgasm takes place, let it come. But don't make yourself uncomfortable in an attempt to have orgasm. With comfort, orgasm will happen naturally.

Schedule three sessions, starting out together, as usual, but again, if only one of you is having difficulty reaching orgasm, that partner may wish to schedule additional individual sessions. Prepare for each session as usual, doing whatever it takes to get you in the mood. If you are having a joint session, begin it by spending some pleasant time together before separating. Whether you are having a joint or individual session, stimulate your genitals once you are in separate rooms. This time keep track of how long you are able to stroke your genitals comfortably; your target is thirty minutes.

Even if you can stimulate your genitals comfortably only for a few minutes or even seconds, don't be concerned. Regular practice will lead to longer periods of sustained comfort. Simply try to remain comfortable for as long as possible. Use lotions or oils if they make you more comfortable.

Each time you stimulate your genitals, try to do it comfortably for slightly longer than your previous time. Choose small enough increases so you don't make yourself uncomfortable by expecting too much. As with most new activities, you are bound to progess slowly at times. It's important for you to find a comfortable rate for your progress. At times, you will probably feel that you are not progressing and at other times you will probably find yourself making big jumps. Do whatever is most comfortable for you. If stimulating your genitals is relatively easy, shoot for five-minute increases. If you seem to be struggling, go for only a thirty-second or one-minute increase. Just do whatever seems right for you.

You may find that you can progress more quickly if you divert your attention away from the self-stimulation. You may find that your body will perform more naturally if you become involved in a second activity at the same time, maybe watching television or reading. Getting involved in something else may help you to relax and at the same time allow you to react to the stimulation more naturally.

If you become uncomfortable, do imagination exercises or change what you're doing. If you can eliminate the discomfort quickly, consider the whole time as sustained comfort. No matter what, learning to eliminate discomfort and create comfort is your goal.

If you are having a joint session, rejoin your partner in the usual room at the agreed-upon time. While in the same room, participate in any of your earlier activities, but do not self-stimulate or progress to orgasm.

Since progress through this assignment can sometimes be frustrating, it is very important that you continue to reward yourselves. These rewards will keep both of you motivated.

When you both are able to comfortably stimulate your genitals for two consecutive thirty-minute sessions or reach orgasm, you have completed this section. If you both are able to have satisfying orgasms, go on to Step 6. If not, read Alternative 4.

ALTERNATIVE 4

The mind is extremely powerful. Thoughts can either bring or prevent success. Positive thoughts are especially important for normal bodily functions over which we have little direct control—such as sleep or orgasm. Thoughts that help you believe you can have and enjoy orgasm will lead you to doing just that.

In this case, it's sexual fantasies that can provide the necessary support. Being able to enjoy your sexual fantasies more freely may provide the help you need to reach orgasm. As your fantasies grow more vivid, you will find your excitement growing by leaps and bounds. As the excitement grows, orgasm should follow.

Take a moment and think about your ability to have sexual fantasies. Do you have any? Are they vivid? Do they create any sexual excitement for you? If not, you may be restricting yourself too much. Even if they do excite you, you might want to free them up even more. The more you can feel your fantasies, the more excitement you will feel. And the more excitement you feel, the more likely you will enjoy orgasm.

You probably already have some fantasies that you can build upon. Get yourself relaxed and begin to concentrate. As you imagine a scene, try to see it in as much detail as you can. Let yourself experience the feelings related to what you're seeing. As you let the feelings grow, you might even find yourself getting excited and find your body responding sexually. If that happens, stay with your fantasy and let your emotions and body do what they want.

You might also want to develop some new fantasies. Plan some specific ways for doing this, like going to an X-rated movie, looking at some sexy magazines, reading a romantic novel, going window shopping for sexy clothes or reading a book such as

Nancy Friday's *My Secret Garden*, which describes women's sexual fantasies. You might even want to talk to your partner or a close friend and learn about other people's fantasies you might use for yourself. By acknowledging your feelings and fantasies, you will probably feel better about yourself and your activities.

You might even have some fantasies about self-stimulation that you would like to attempt but haven't yet tried. Don't forget that sex can be fun and that it should not be pressured. Try to figure out what will put a little more zest into your sessions alone. You might want to try a new place, a new style of self-stimulation or a new atmosphere. The list of possible changes or additions goes on and on.

After you have developed some pleasant fantasies, again schedule three sessions with your partner. Before a session starts, heighten your fantasies as much as possible. At the scheduled time, begin the session by gradually progressing through the kissing and caressing stages. If you both want to, share your fantasies. You may or may not find it more stimulating to share your fantasies with your partner. At a mutually agreeable time, separate.

Now that you're alone, begin by thinking of any fantasy that turns you on. Try to make it seem so real that you can feel what you are imagining. Make it come to life. When you feel ready, begin to stimulate your body, including your genitals. Try to make your self-stimulation a part of your fantasy. As your hand glides over your body, let your fantasies take over. Continue this self-stimulation session for at least thirty minutes. If orgasm takes place comfortably, let it come. But do not force yourself to have orgasm. With sustained comfort, orgasm will happen naturally.

During these sessions, if you are the wife, try to contract and release your pelvic-floor muscles several times (as described in the exercises on pages 85 to 87). Try these contractions at appropriate times during the fantasies and especially during times of physical excitement. Building the exercises into a fantasy may be extremely arousing.

At the agreed-upon time, get back with your partner, ending the session doing things you enjoy together. However, once back together, do not self-stimulate or progress to orgasm. If you want to self-stimulate again, go through the same process of separating and then rejoining once more.

Try three sessions like the one described. If you like what is happening and want more sessions, go ahead. If you were both able to have satisfying orgasms during two consecutive sessions, go on to Step 6. If you still have difficulty, read Alternative 5.

ALTERNATIVE 5

Orgasms often bring on what seems like very strange behavior. People may yell, scream or moan. Their bodies perspire, grow rigid, and jerk and twist uncontrollably. Since you are having difficulty reaching orgasm, it may mean that you are uncomfortable with this kind of behavior. If you are, you may simply need to learn to loosen up.

Your new assignment is to learn to become comfortable with the behavior that accompanies an orgasm, which you will do by acting as if you were having an orgasm. By following the directions and practicing often, getting loose will become much easier and, quite likely, orgasm will too. When you feel comfortable acting out an orgasm, you will see if your acting has paid off by scheduling some regular self-stimulation sessions.

First, schedule three sessions together for each of you to act out an orgasm. You might, but you don't have to, begin the sessions by enjoying any of the earlier steps of closeness. You might both want to simply go ahead and act out having an orgasm. Do your acting either undressed or partially dressed. The partner having less difficulty should act first, while the other partner reads aloud the instructions below. After the first partner is done, reverse the roles.

When you are both ready, the acting partner should lie down in a comfortable place, most likely the bed, and the other partner should begin to read the instructions aloud. The instructions should be read with long pauses so that the acting partner can really experience what's happening. The person acting out the instructions should attempt to follow them as closely as possible, exaggerating everything in order to actually feel the emotions and the body's responses. When you're the performer, fantasize that you actually are having an orgasm.

Since this loosening up is a new activity, don't be

surprised if you have difficulty at first. You might even feel embarrassed, silly, dumb or any of a number of other things. (If you break up laughing at first, that's OK.) While this activity may be uncomfortable at first, it should be extremely helpful, and it's important that you try it just as described below. The more you try it, the easier it will become and if you can really get into it, you might even find yourself liking it. But if you should encounter discomfort, signal your partner immediately. You might find that gradually increasing the exaggeration or just extreme exaggeration of one step will help get you through the discomfort.

If you are each able to remain comfortable during your first acting experience, try doing it twice more during that session. But if discomfort arises, rest for a few moments until you are comfortable. When the discomfort fades, try again. If the discomfort doesn't fade, talk over any concerns with your partner. Your lover will probably be able to provide some needed emotional support.

INSTRUCTIONS FOR ACTING OUT AN ORGASM

1. Lie on your back with your hands at your sides and your palms down.
2. Close your eyes.
3. With your eyes still closed, frequently pull your eyelids even tighter.
4. Take a few deep breaths which are big and noisy.

5. Begin to slide your hands on the surface beneath you, keeping your palms flat on the surface.
6. Increase the movement of your arms by using more shoulder motion.
7. Start sliding your legs from side to side.
8. Move your legs more by bending your knees to move your legs up and down.
9. Accelerate your breathing.
10. Move your hips back and forth in a circular motion.
11. Exaggerate all of your movements a little more by moving your arms and legs in larger circular motions.
12. Begin to move your head, back and pelvic muscles.
13. Continue to squirm in the same place so that your whole body is moving.
14. Let your entire body jerk frequently.
15. Let your pelvic area thrust up and down.
16. Plant your feet so that you can use your legs to help you thrust.
17. As you breathe faster, also breathe more deeply.
18. Let your fingers and toes begin to curl.
19. Begin to stroke your body, especially your genital area.
20. Push down with your hands on your pelvic area as you thrust forward.
21. Be aware that you may have a feeling that you are holding back urine flow.

22. Make grunting noises.
23. Thrust harder and harder as your hands push down on your pelvic area.
24. Begin to contort your face by pulling your jaw tighter and your forehead down as your facial muscles pull tighter.
25. Begin to pull your genital muscles tight so you feel that you are holding back urine.
26. Begin to make shorter and faster thrusts.
27. Feel your back and neck muscles pulling tighter.
28. Feel your genitals not wanting to stop their motion.
29. Make louder noises; scream.
30. Make still harder thrusting motions.
31. Thrust forward and feel that your genitals are ready to explode.
32. Thrust a few more times while all the tension in your body does explode.
33. Sense the release of tension throughout your body.
34. Enjoy a feeling of total relaxation after your genitals seem to have let go.
35. Let your breathing slow down as you begin to feel all worn out.
36. As your movements slow down and finally stop, and as your arms and legs become still, simply lie quietly.

When you have completed your three acting-out sessions, schedule three regular sessions. Begin them as usual by enjoying being together. When you're both ready, separate. Each of you should stimulate yourself until you reach orgasm or for at least thirty minutes. Use a lubricant and any skills you have developed. In particular, use your imagination to fantasize enjoying any sexual activities. If both of you are able to have satisfying orgasms during two consecutive self-stimulation sessions, proceed to Step 6. If you continue to have difficulty, read Alternative 6.

ALTERNATIVE 6

Sex takes time. When people feel pressured to hurry, they often run into trouble. Like taking a test or falling asleep, sex, if you put a time limit on it, becomes more difficult. This is especially true when people have concerns about how they're going to perform. Frequently, people who are having trouble reaching orgasm simply are not allowing themselves enough time to enjoy the emotions associated with sexual activities. Once they become easily orgasmic and gain confidence, "quickies" or "nooners" often become a real pleasure.

All too often people in our society tightly schedule their lives because of commitments to work, school, community, family or other activities. Often these commitments seem absolutely unavoidable or necessary, and it feels as if there's no way to cut back on them. As a result, couples set aside only a limited amount of time in their daily lives for sex. This may be fifteen minutes, a half-hour or an hour a day (or every week, or whatever). Although this may seem to be plenty of time, in reality it may not be enough time for *you* to truly enjoy a range of emotions.

When their time is limited, people have to have sex quickly, including getting aroused and reaching orgasm. But they often find that their bodies and emotions don't respond as quickly as they'd like. Instead, their bodies seem to want to respond slowly and let their emotions build. Their bodies appear not to want to be rushed. Couples in this situation often find that time limits lead to dissatisfaction with their sex life.

Setting aside enough time to let your body enjoy sex and perform as it wants is a *must*. You might want to consider scheduling large blocks of time for several sexual sessions—as much as an afternoon or an evening for each session. You may not need all this time, but you will want to allow your body plenty of time to enjoy what is happening. Old habits are difficult to break, so you may need to make a conscious effort to make sure you don't schedule too tightly. As your body begins to function as you would like it to, you will gradually be able to decrease the amount of time you need.

Schedule three sessions again, but with one big difference: *allow plenty of time* for yourselves to enjoy each session. These will not be much different from previous sessions except that they will be a lot longer. During the sessions, feel free to do what you want during shared time and individual time. Do what feels good to you. Don't rush yourself. If you want to stop, stop. Just relax and take it easy. Remember that sex is fun and sex is emotional. Give yourself the chance to feel it and enjoy it.

Before the session begins, you may want to do some preparation. Start early enough so that you can do everything you'd like without feeling rushed. At the designated time, begin the session by lying next to each other. Gradually progress to kissing and petting. Take all the time you need. You may want to add something new—a bath for two or a pillow fight, maybe. When you're ready, go into different rooms. Stay as long as you want and do whatever you want. You might even want to rejoin and separate several times.

While in a separate room, begin to caress your body, including your genitals. Start and stop whenever you like. However, before the session ends, try to massage your gentials for at least forty-five minutes during one separation. During these sessions, try to set your fantasies free. Give yourself the chance to let your emotions flow. If orgasm happens comfortably, let it come. But don't make yourself uncomfortable in an attempt to have an orgasm. Orgasm will happen when you are comfortable enough.

It may take a lot of time to get excited and reach orgasm. Don't worry, these responses will come faster with time and practice. Simply enjoy what feels good to you now. By giving yourself plenty of time to enjoy what is happening and by giving yourself permission to enjoy it, your body will slowly begin to learn to perform as you want.

Schedule three long sessions like this, allowing yourselves plenty of time. If you both are able to have satisfying orgasm during two consecutive sessions, proceed to Step 6. If not, read Alternative 7.

ALTERNATIVE 7

Manual stimulation may just not be enough to get you started. Maybe a little mechanical assistance will provide the stimulation you need. A vibrator can be a lot of fun and even if you are already having orgasms, you may want to experiment.

Before your next session, purchase a battery-operated "facial" vibrator that resembles a penis. This type of vibrator costs about ten dollars and can be purchased at most drug stores. You may be a little embarrassed about buying one, but don't worry; it is well worth it. (Keep in mind that the reason they are so easy to find in the drug stores is that the stores sell lots of them. It's just another item of merchandise for them.) You will probably soon be wondering why you didn't get one sooner. In fact, you may find that you each want to have your own personal vibrator.

Schedule three more sessions, but if only one of you is having difficulty reaching satisfying orgasm, you may also want to have several individual sessions. Before you begin a session, go through your standard ritual to get into the mood. At the designated time, if it's a session together, begin the session by simply enjoying being together. Hug, kiss, talk or do whatever you want. Then, at a mutually agreed-upon time, separate. While in separate rooms, each of you is to self-stimulate, one (or both) of you using a vibrator, for as long as comfortable.

When the two of you have separated and you're ready, turn on the vibrator and apply it to your genitals with a fairly soft touch. Gently move it around, exploring all the sensitive areas of and near your genitals. The wife should explore both in and around her vagina, but she will probably find that the most pleasurable areas are near her clitoris. She probably will find that direct contact with the clitoris results in too much stimulation. The husband should explore areas both on and around his penis and scrotum. He should also explore the area just behind his scrotum between his legs. He will probably find that using the vibrator on the underside of his penis provides the most pleasurable sensation. Whichever of you is using the vibrator, you should try different strokes, speeds and pressures to find out what you enjoy best. If you reach orgasm comfortably, let it come, but do not push yourself uncomfortably in an attempt to have orgasm. With sustained comfort, orgasm will simply happen.

Try to prolong the amount of time that you are able to use the vibrator on your genitals without discomfort, but if you become uncomfortable, stop or use it on another part of your body. Start again when you've gotten rid of the discomfort. If you tend to become irritated by prolonged use of the vibrator, use a lubricant.

Don't be surprised if it's necessary for you to massage your genitals with the vibrator for as long as forty-five minutes before you really start to feel pleasure.

And don't be surprised if the area of pleasurable sensitivity shifts throughout the session. Simply try to find the most enjoyable places to stroke and allow your body to respond freely. Both of you may find that contracting your pelvic muscles will help increase the sensitivity in your genitals.

After you have both finished your individual stimulating, rejoin your partner. Participate in any activities of closeness that you both like, but don't self-stimulate or progress to orgasm while you're together. If you want to self-stimulate some more, separate again and rejoin afterwards.

If you are successful in using the vibrator to reach orgasm, you will want to gradually wean yourself from it so you can also reach orgasm through manual stimulation. This is easy; just use the vibrator and your hand simultaneously and then intermittently.

Begin by using the vibrator to stimulate your genitals, then, simultaneously, use your other hand to stimulate yourself, caressing and massaging your body wherever it feels good. Try to increase using your hand while maintaining pleasure. You may want to begin by using your hand to massage parts of your body other than your genitals and then, when you're comfortable, begin to stimulate your genitals.

When you begin to feel excited, temporarily turn off (or hold away) the vibrator, but continue to massage your genitals with your hands. Use the vibrator only occasionally to heighten your excitement. Attempt to bring yourself to orgasm using only your hands. If you find that you need the vibrator to reach orgasm, use it and your hands simultaneously just before and during orgasm. If possible, switch to using only your hands to massage your genitals just as you are about to reach orgasm.

Continue to alternately massage your genitals with the vibrator and your hands, relying less and less on the vibrator and more on your hands. As you grow more comfortable reaching orgasm this way, try to decrease the length of time that you use the vibrator while you increase the use of your hands.

Don't be surprised if this step takes a long time. This assignment often takes longer than any other in this book. Make sure you schedule sessions often. Keep trying even if it becomes difficult at times. Your success in the two final steps is built in large part on your success and the ability you've achieved in this chapter. Remember, too, to reward yourself and your partner after every five sessions that you attempt, even when these include sessions alone. It is very important that you keep trying and that you both feel rewarded for your efforts.

If both of you are able to reach satisfying orgasm through manual stimulation, proceed to the next step. If you are able to reach orgasm through the use of the vibrator, but not manually, have a few more sessions to continue to wean yourself from the vibrator and then advance to the next step. If one or both of you is still not enjoying satisfying orgasms after three sessions, read Alternative 8.

ALTERNATIVE 8

Since you are reading this section, one or both of you must be having difficulty either in reaching orgasm or in reaching orgasms that are satisfying.

If you're having trouble reaching orgasm at all, you might want to talk to your doctor. It is possible that what you are encountering is caused by a medical problem or medications. Sometimes a solution is very easy.

If you are having orgasms but they are not satisfying, it's possible that the problem is physical, but more likely that it's psychological. Although reaching orgasm is something to feel good about, some people don't. Instead, they feel guilty, sad or anxious, or have no feeling at all during or after an orgasm. It's as if it were not OK to enjoy all the pleasures of orgasm.

In the simplest terms, you are probably restricting either the behavior or the sensations of orgasm. Since you have most likely learned this restriction, you can just as easily unlearn it.

Because you may not know what an uncontrolled orgasm is like, you may be afraid that your behavior would be, by your standards, too bizarre. If you're afraid of what might happen during an orgasm, you may be trying to avoid "undesirable" feelings or behavior and thus unconsciously blocking some of the feelings that accompany an orgasm. To really enjoy orgasm, you need to let your behavior just happen—to give up control over your body and emotions, and let your body take over. If this kind of restriction is hampering you, you'll need more practice letting your body respond naturally. (For comparison, think again about falling asleep. You can't force yourself to fall asleep; you can only let yourself fall asleep naturally.) Go back to the instructions for acting out an orgasm and practice them at least three more times.

If it's your emotions that are causing the restriction, you may have some concerns that are getting in the way. For example, you might feel disappointed with your orgasms because you believe them to be inferior to what's described by your friends or by books. Or you might be afraid that sex will lead to something undesirable such as an unwanted pregnancy or the troubles of an earlier bad relationship. Or you might be trying to meet someone else's standards such as having sex with only one partner during a lifetime or only within narrow rules such as place or frequency. You need to learn that sex *is* good. It's as simple as that.

Nature has provided us with the ability to have orgasms and you have the right to enjoy yours. Now you need to learn to accept that right. Only you have the right to decide how much sexual pleasure you will enjoy.

By continuing to regularly reach orgasm, you will gradually learn to accept the pleasure. Remember that orgasm is not always memorable or earth-shattering. You will be able to watch your pleasure gradually increase. You may still be nervous about it, but the bad feelings should gradually decrease and the day will come when you will have no reservations at all about the pleasure of reaching orgasm.

Give yourself permission to enjoy! Until you feel good about your orgasms, give yourself that permission three times a day. Say to yourself, "I have the right to enjoy my orgasm and I am going to enjoy it." Say it right now. Develop as much enthusiasm as you can. When you start to feel good about your orgasms, congratulate and encourage yourself. Say to yourself, "I feel good about that experience," and don't forget to tell your partner. By encouraging yourself this way you might even learn to enjoy orgasms quickly, but more likely it will take time for the inhibiting feelings to fade away. Once you have gotten past these obstacles, give yourself a well-earned reward and proceed to Step 6.

But if, even with the most determined and conscientious practicing, you can't reach orgasm through self-stimulation, you might want to consult a qualified counselor.

CHAPTER 12

Step 6: Fun and Fantasy

NEW lovers create a special excitement in their lives. From the morning alarm to the goodnight kiss, the magic of the relationship turns mundane routines into special events. You see it in their eyes and bodies, and hear it in their conversation. And you just know that their sex life is exciting.

The next time you're in a romantic restaurant, look at the other people. You can easily spot couples in love and those who just co-exist together. Couples in love will be constantly touching one another, talking, laughing and waiting for their partner's next pearl of wisdom. Couples who just co-exist with each other will be seldom talking and may look as if they could just as easily be eating alone, although if you listen hard enough you may hear one of them politely ask, "How's your meal?"

Gradually losing some of the novelty and excitement of a new relationship is normal and is to be expected. Some reduction of sexual desire and activity is also normal. But losing too much can be extremely harmful to a marriage. To keep sex special, couples ought to continue to expect a little bit of magic, and then make sure it happens.

Keeping a couple's love life alive and well is a life-long challenge. Because marital and personal stresses tempt couples to put off sexual activity and pleasure, too often they'll find themselves reducing their sexual activities—in and out of the bedroom. Instead of hugging, holding, kissing and caressing at any time of day, sexual activity becomes synonymous with intercourse. And, when their sexual activity becomes so limited, their sexual pleasure suffers. At that point, many couples discover that attempting to turn sexual emotions on and off just for bedroom activities becomes too complicated. Instead of more desire resulting from less frequent sex, the opposite happens: they aren't able to get turned on sexually when they want to. Many couples further complicate the problem by focusing on sexual performance instead of pleasure, and as performance grows in importance, sex becomes more like a job than pleasure. Taking sex so seriously takes the joy out of it. Worse, when people worry about their sexual functioning, their fears often turn into reality.

The special ingredient that makes life—and sex—special for most new lovers is playfulness. Much of a marriage is not aimed at accomplishing anything in particular except simply enjoying each other's company. This is particularly true with sex—it is simply a way for two people to share their love, emotional pleasure and physical pleasure.

Making sex playful can add a richness to your love life. Instead of worrying about your sexual frustrations or goals, you will be thinking about ways to make your love life more fun.

Playfulness isn't so much what you do, but how you do it. Almost anything can be fun if you want it to be. With sex, playfulness is simply what you have been doing during your practice sessions so far— caring, sharing, building optimism and a feeling of not being rushed—but carried one step further.

Playfulness is any fun that you both enjoy—with the emphasis on both. So stretch your imagination and your confidence and allow plenty of time to enjoy the sexual activities that you both like. Put the problems of the day behind you and focus on making each moment pleasurable for the two of you. Forget about goals and simply enjoy what's happening. Think about finding some way of making each session special—not necessarily anything expensive or elaborate, just a change to make it more interesting.

Welcome to your new assignment, which for many people is their favorite: arousing your lover to orgasm through any method that you both want *other* than intercourse. Playfulness and fantasy will be your approach.

Think back to when you were new lovers, when sex was fresh and exciting. In particular, think about the things you did that were fun. You'll probably remember times that you haven't thought of in years. You'll probably also recall that the way you enjoyed sex was a lot different then. Most likely you were more adventurous, tolerant and playful. If it was fun back then, maybe it would be fun now.

Your greatest aphrodisiac, by far, is your imagination. Give yourself permission to enjoy your sexual fantasies, dreams and desires at any time of day. They are normal and we all have them. Just by giving yourself the right to enjoy your fantasies, you will find them growing in number and sensuality. If you need help freeing up your fantasies (or even if you begin to get too serious about sex), you will probably find that the simplest way to start is to take a break from your usual routine. Do it with your lover. Together, let yourselves put aside your daily lives once in a while and enjoy a change of pace. It doesn't need to be a lot of time, just a pleasure break for the two of you. Take a walk along a quiet path or have a drink in a secluded place where you can share the atmosphere without distraction. Try a peaceful stroll along a beach, an intimate dinner or a snuggle near a fire. If you have the time, take a trip that you will both find romantic.

As your fantasies grow, pay close attention to what turns you on. Keep a mental note of what situations, actions, words, thoughts, feelings and touches lead to your sexual arousal. Don't expect anyone else, especially your lover, to have the same desires. Men and women tend to have very different fantasies. For example, men are more likely to be turned on by visual sexiness while many women prefer fantasies that focus more on emotional closeness. No matter what turns you on, encourage it. Finally, give yourself and your partner the encouragement and permission to indulge in the pleasure of arousing each other's fantasies.

Ideally, you have been building romance into your lives outside of the bedroom as you have been progressing through this course, so that hugging, holding, kissing and caressing are already a regular part of your day. Flowers, cards, unscheduled phone calls and a loving atmosphere are becoming a part of your special events and practice sessions. Now is the time to take all this one step further and develop a playful atmosphere that leads to sexual arousal.

Each of you will share with your partner your fantasies and what you've learned in the last sessions about what specifically turns you on. Armed with this information, you each face the challenge of exciting your lover. Be creative and give your lover the winning combination of caring, love and great pleasure.

Just before starting each session, spend a few minutes together discussing your fantasies and briefly describing what turns you on physically. As you both describe what arouses you, pay attention to what especially excites your lover and think of great ways to use that information. It may be something as simple as a particular touch or as elaborate as sharing a romantic and loving evening as a prelude to the session. You might find it exciting to act as if you were just meeting for the first time. Although you may be thinking that fantasies need to be something unusual, don't rule out slow, gentle love-making with lots of holding and caressing as a stimulating fantasy.

When you schedule your three practice sessions, select places that will be as conducive as possible to your fantasies. You may want to create a mood in your own bedroom, or you may prefer to get away to a motel, a hot tub or a secluded cabin. Arrange for anything that will add to your fantasies: sexy clothes, home videos, magazines, a bottle of champagne or whatever. If the two of you have fantasies that are completely different, you may want to go with one partner's fantasies for one session and the other partner's fantasies the next.

Begin the session with some serious necking. Try any sexual stimulation other than intercourse to gently arouse the sexual passion within each of you. As you both begin to feel the excitement, one of you should begin to share your findings from the self-discovery sessions. Be specific. Show your lover how to arouse you and let it happen. Remember that your partner can't read your mind—you have to explain where and how you want to be caressed. Stroke and caress yourself the way you like it and when your partner understands, let your partner begin to take over. Continue to tell your partner how to make the caressing increasingly stimulating. Keep going to the point of orgasm if it occurs comfortably. Afterward, switch roles.

While you are being aroused, let your partner hear and see your enjoyment. As your partner follows your instructions, talk about the pleasures you're feeling. If you would like something different be specific and positive in your directions. Let your arousal excite your body naturally. Allow yourself to squirm, moan or do whatever your body tells you to do. Don't worry about embarrassment—the more unrestricted your body's response, the more you and your partner will enjoy it.

Finally, allow your growing sexual excitement to help you return the pleasure you're receiving. Giving your lover an orgasm can be just as gratifying as having one yourself. When you are the one doing the arousing, make your lover feel special. No matter what else you do, always keep your lover at the center of your attention. Feel free to be creative, but always stay within the limits set by your partner. Allow yourself to grow aroused, but when you're the giver, avoid getting more aroused than your partner and stealing the show.

For both of you the rule during these practice sessions is to keep things as light and as much fun as possible. Although your aim is sexual arousal, your immediate goal is pleasure. Turn your imaginations loose, let go of your inhibitions and allow your fantasies to seem real. Great pleasure will come as your imaginations stimulate your minds and your bodies.

As you allow your fantasies and sexual pleasure to grow, use all of your senses to heighten your excitement. Be aware that imagination can be much more powerful than reality. You should have plenty of your own ideas about stimulating your senses and imagination, but here are a few for starters.

HEARING

Discover what sounds make you think about sex. Maybe a favorite song or breaking waves arouse your amorous drives. Talking about sex or even talking "dirty" may do it. Perhaps silence with occasional sounds of arousal may be even more stimulating. At any time, hearing your partner say that you are attractive and desirable will add to the pleasure.

TOUCHING

Touching, of course, usually provides the most stimulation and is the most fun. Stroking your lover's genitals at home in bed creates a lot of pleasure, but stroking your lover's genitals discreetly in an unexpected situation can certainly create a response. For example, stroking your lover's genitals and thigh under a restaurant table (even with your foot) may get quite a reaction. Try it while riding in a car, under a beach blanket, or in a taxi.

TASTING

Tasting is an exciting part of intimacy. Don't forget to nibble on your partner's neck, ears and breasts. Try adding a little more flavor by spreading jam, peanut butter or whipped cream over your partner's body and then licking it off. Share a drink of your favorite liqueur to make you feel more relaxed and amorous.

SEEING

Sexy clothes or a sexy body have been good turn-ons throughout recorded history. Surprising your lover by wearing something totally different than your usual style can be a turn-on. For example, if you usually dress conservatively, try turning up in a restaurant wearing something outlandish. What you don't see can be as exciting as what you do see. During a party, try whispering to your partner that you're not wearing any underwear. This will probably keep your partner's attention for the rest of the evening. Try sex with the lights on, or if that's what you always do, with the lights off.

SMELL

Obviously, perfumes, colognes and aftershaves can be arousing. Sometimes personal body odors can be turn-ons. Candles, flowers and other common fragrances can add to the whole sexual atmosphere.

Once the two of you have become comfortable stimulating each other to orgasm, try doing it to each other simultaneously. Use the same techniques you've been using, and enjoy the pleasure of arousing each other at the same time. Try whatever the two of you want, *except* for intercourse.

If at any time during the sessions either of you feels uncomfortable, remember to signal your discomfort immediately and suggest a remedy. If that doesn't work, take a break for a few minutes. When you feel comfortable, begin again. As you are exciting each other, it's possible that at least one of you will want to try oral sex, but if this causes you discomfort, let your lover know. Since this is often a stumbling block for couples, it needs to be faced directly.

Remember that throughout this course you have been learning to enjoy the pleasures of the moment. Along the way you both have learned to enjoy sexual activities that you may not have enjoyed in the past. Don't assume that your partner still disapproves of an activity just because your partner disapproved of it in the past. You may be surprised to find out how much you both can now enjoy something you didn't enjoy before.

Schedule your three practice sessions and decide now where you'll have them. If both of you are able to reach orgasm during two consecutive sessions, go on to Step 7. If you both want more practice, feel free to schedule more sessions. However, if at any time after the three sessions, one or both of you feels you are not making progress, read Alternative 1. No matter how well you are progressing, continue to reward yourselves after every five sessions.

Remember, discomfort is any uneasiness. Here's the discomfort list to refresh your memory of things to watch for in this assignment. You are having discomfort if you feel:

- Anxious, nervous, afraid, up tight, edgy, or angry;

- Too hot, too cold, or aware of any other form of physical discomfort;
- Guilty, ashamed or disgusted;
- Rushed or pressured;
- Compelled to attempt something not prescribed by the program or not wanting to attempt something that had been prescribed;
- That your body responded unpleasantly or not at all. (For example, did you experience pain, tight muscles, loss of erection, reaching orgasm before you want, having difficulty reaching orgasm, having unsatisfying orgasm or having pain?)

ALTERNATIVE 1

If you've had difficulty exciting one another, don't get discouraged. With a little practice, you should be able to create the fun that this assignment should be.

Your aim is still to excite each other to orgasm through any mutually agreeable method *other* than intercourse. Since you've encountered some kind of difficulty, you may not be signalling discomfort soon enough. Learning to acknowledge the discomfort quickly and to propose a solution will help you succeed.

Begin each session as before, with a good location and a romantic mood. Take all the time you want to get yourself ready, but be in the appointed place on time, all set to go. Begin slowly by doing some hugging, hand-holding, caressing and necking. After a few minutes, one of you should begin to sexually arouse the other and even try to engage in whatever produced discomfort. Give each other instructions to bring on the discomfort. Since you are creating this situation, you will be able to identify the discomfort as soon as it begins and signal immediately.

When you signal discomfort, give your partner specific *positive* instructions such as "Touch me here, but very softly." Avoid any blaming or negative statements; "You're doing the wrong thing" is not the approach you want. If you don't know why you became uncomfortable, return to hugging, hand-holding, caressing and kissing. When the discomfort fades, try again to get uncomfortable, figure out what the problem is and eliminate the discomfort. Continue this until you both feel that you can signal discomfort immediately and get comfortable again or until you realize that continuing this exercise is fruitless.

Do this special assignment for at least three sessions. If you successfully eliminate discomfort, enjoy arousing each other as long as you both want. On the other hand, if this alternative isn't the answer, move on to Alternative 2.

ALTERNATIVE 2

Apparently, some part of arousing each other continues to cause you discomfort. A good way to replace discomfort with comfort, arousal and orgasm is by using your imagination. You can learn to enjoy doing something in reality, if you can be comfortable imagining doing it. The more pleasurable it is in your imagination, the more pleasurable it will be in reality.

This time, instead of practice sessions together, the partner who is feeling discomfort should plan four individual ten-minute sessions to take place in the next few days. During the sessions alone, this partner will practice using imagination to create and eliminate discomfort. Find a comfortable chair where you can lean back, put your feet up and relax. Close your eyes, take a few deep breaths, and feel your body slowing down. When you feel relatively peaceful, imagine a very pleasant scene such as lying on a beach after swimming, feeling the warmth of the sun or engaging in something you really enjoy doing. Try to picture this scene as completely as possible and enjoy the emotions associated with it. If you really stretch your imagination, it should be almost as good as being there.

When you are able to vividly imagine yourself in this scene for one minute, end it and imagine yourself either exciting your lover or being excited by your lover. Try to feel all of the emotions. Enjoy the pleasure and acknowledge the discomfort. Try to experience the discomfort. As soon as you begin to feel it, end this practice scene and return to the pleasant one until the discomfort goes away. Continue this process for the ten-minute session. Each time you imagine yourself involved in mutual stimulation try to feel a little more of the pleasure than the previous time. Little by little you will find yourself working through the discomfort and finding the pleasure instead.

After at least four imagery sessions alone, schedule three arousal sessions together. If you become uncomfortable during a session, signal your partner and suggest a solution. To help reduce your discomfort during the sessions, bring back the pleasant scene in your imagination. As soon as you are comfortable again, continue the arousal. Whenever discomfort returns, create the pleasant imagery.

If you're successful in eliminating discomfort during the practice sessions, go on to Step 7. If discomfort continues, read Alternative 3.

ALTERNATIVE 3

People are often unable to reach orgasm simply because their genitals have not been stimulated long enough. They may think that it shouldn't take so long, but in fact it often takes longer because the stimulation is a new experience for them. While you have grown accustomed to reaching orgasm by stimulating your own genitals, you now need to grow accustomed to reaching orgasm in front of your lover. For this assignment, your aim will be to comfortably stimulate each other's genitals simultaneously for thirty minutes. As you maintain comfort for prolonged periods of time, sexual excitement will grow and orgasm will follow. If orgasm is reached comfortably, let it happen. But don't make yourself uncomfortable trying. Orgasm will happen naturally, remember, once you can become and stay comfortable.

Schedule three sessions as usual. If only one of you is having difficulty reaching orgasm, you may want to dedicate the sessions to arousing that partner. Prepare for each session as usual, doing whatever it takes to get in the mood and beginning each session by kissing, holding, hugging or doing whatever you both want. When you're both ready, begin as you did in the past sessions. This time keep track of how long you are each able to remain comfortable as your genitals are caressed (and as you caress your partner's). You are aiming for either thirty minutes of stimulation or orgasm.

Even if you can remain comfortable for only a few minutes or even seconds while your genitals are being stimulated (or while you are stimulating your partner), don't be concerned. Regular practice will lead to longer periods of sustained comfort. Simply try to remain comfortable for as long as possible. Use lotions or oils or whatever will help to make you more comfortable.

Each time your partner stimulates your genitals, try to remain comfortable for slightly longer than the last time. Choose small enough increases that you don't cause yourself discomfort by expecting too much. As with most new activities, you need to progress slowly at times, and it's important to find a comfortable rate for you. At times you will probably feel that you are moving ahead slowly and at other times you will probably find yourself making big leaps in both time and arousal. Do whatever is most comfortable for you to keep up your progress. If having your genitals stimulated is relatively easy, aim for five-minute increases. However, if you seem to be struggling, go for only a thirty-second or one-minute increase. Just do whatever seems right for you.

You may find that your body will perform more naturally if you're involved in something else at the same time—possibly getting lost in your fantasies, or exciting your lover. Some people enjoy watching television or reading while their genitals are stimulated. Getting involved in doing something else may help you relax and simultaneously allow you to respond more naturally to the stimulation.

If discomfort arises, acknowledge it immediately, and eliminate it either by using your imagination exercises or by changing the activity. If you can eliminate the discomfort quickly, consider the whole session as enjoying sustained comfort. No matter what, learning to eliminate any discomfort and recreating comfort is of utmost importance.

When you are both able to be comfortable while your genitals are stimulated for thirty minutes or reach orgasm for two consecutive sessions, you are ready to move on. If you both are able to attain satisfying orgasms, move to Step 7. If not, read Alternative 4. Since progress through this assignment can sometimes be frustrating, it is very important that you

continue with your rewards to keep yourselves motivated, changing the rewards as often as you want.

ALTERNATIVE 4

If manual stimulation isn't quite enough to get
you started maybe what you need is a little mechanical
assistance. Using a vibrator can be a lot of fun—
exciting, too. Even if you are already having orgasms,
you might want to experiment with it for even more
fun.

Before your next session, if you have not already
gotten one, buy a battery-operated "facial" vibrator—
the kind that resembles a penis. As noted before, they
cost about ten dollars and can be bought at most drug
stores. If you're a little embarrassed to buy one, go to a
part of town where no one knows you—but in any
case do it. You'll probably soon be wondering why you
didn't get one earlier. You may even want more than
one.

Again schedule three practice sessions. If only
one of you is having difficulty reaching orgasm, you
may want to spend most of the time in each session
dedicated to the arousal of that one partner. Before
you begin a session, go through your standard get-in-
the-mood ritual. Then, at the designated time, begin
by simply enjoying being together. Hug, kiss, talk or do
whatever you both want.

At a mutually agreeable time, begin the sexual arousal. The person doing the arousing should turn on the vibrator and apply it to the other partner's genitals with a fairly soft touch. Gently move it around, exploring all the sensitive areas on and near the genitals. On the woman, explore areas both in and around the vagina, although the most pleasurable areas will probably be those areas near her clitoris. However, she will most likely find that direct contact with her clitoris itself results in too much stimulation. On the man, explore both on and around his penis and scrotum. Also explore the area just behind his scrotum, between his legs. The husband will probably find that stimulation on the underside of his penis provides the most pleasurable sensation. For both of you, try different strokes, speeds and pressures to find the feelings you like best. If orgasm happens comfortably, let it come, but don't try to force it. Don't worry, with sustained comfort orgasm will happen whether you think about it or not.

Now try to prolong the amount of time that your partner uses the vibrator on you without discomfort. As before, ask your partner to stop when you become uncomfortable or to use the vibrator on another part of you. Then, when the discomfort has been eliminated, have your partner return the vibrator to your genitals. Use a lubricant if prolonged use of the vibrator tends to cause irritation.

Don't be surprised if it takes as long as forty-five minutes before you really start to feel pleasure. Don't be surprised either if the area of pleasurable sensitivity shifts throughout the sessions. Just try to tell your partner where the most enjoyable areas are and then allow your body to respond freely. Both of you, by the way, may find that contracting your pelvic muscles will help increase the sensitivity in your genitals.

If you're successful using the vibrator to reach orgasm, you will want to wean yourself away from it so that you can eventually reach orgasm through your lover's manual stimulation. You can do this very easily by having your lover use the vibrator and a hand simultaneously and then intermittently.

Your lover begins the weaning process by using the vibrator to stimulate your genitals. Then, still using the vibrator, your lover will begin to use his or her hands to caress your body wherever it feels good. As time goes on, your lover can increase using hands while maintaining those pleasurable feelings. When you begin to feel excited, have your lover temporarily remove the vibrator while continuing to caress your genitals with the fingers. Your lover should attempt to bring you to orgasm using hands only. If you find that you need the vibrator to reach orgasm, have your lover use both the vibrator and a hand simultaneously just before and during your orgasm. If possible, your lover should switch to hands-only stimulation of your genitals when you reach orgasm.

Rely progressively less and less on the vibrator and more and more on your partner's hands. Continue to have your partner alternately stimulate your genitals with the vibrator and then the hands. Gradually try to reach orgasm through hand stimulation alone. As you grow more comfortable with reaching orgasm this way, try to decrease the frequency and length of time with the vibrator while increasing the use of the hands.

Don't be surprised if this step takes some time. Make sure that you schedule sessions often and keep trying even if it sometimes is difficult. And stay with your rewards.

If both of you are able to reach satisfying orgasm through each other's manual stimulation for two consecutive sessions, proceed to the next step. If you are able to reach orgasm through use of the vibrator but not manually, have a few more sessions to continue to wean yourself from the vibrator and then advance to the next step. If one or both of you are not enjoying satisfying orgasms after three sessions, read Alternative 5.

ALTERNATIVE 5

Success with this assignment is necessary to your overall sexual success. The best solution at this time is simply more and more practice. Since you were each able to achieve orgasm through self-stimulation, you will definitely be able to succeed with perseverance. Start this assignment over again, try to make it fun and allow your partner to give you the pleasure of an orgasm.

However, if nothing seems to work, you might consider discussing your problem with a professional counselor.

CHAPTER **13**

Step 7: The Ultimate Sharing

THIS step is about the two big *I*'s. One, as you might guess, is Intercourse. The other is Individuality. They're a lot more closely connected than you may think.

But first let's back up to love-making—for which all of us have highly personal definitions. For some, sex is uncontrollable passion with earth-shaking orgasm. For others it is romance, love, caring, sharing, sensual contact and specific but less dramatic sexual activities. What is really wonderful is that sex can be all of the above.

Although *romantic* love gets the credit for making the world go round, *enduring* love is the real driving force. With romantic love, instead of feeling like two separate individuals, each lover feels like part of an unbeatable team. This is when "Love is blind."

But, as time goes on, each lover begins to see again that they are each distinct individuals no matter how much they have in common. This is when couples need to think about building their deeper and their enduring love, which, unlike romantic love, calls for conscious attention. Lasting love grows as each partner encourages the other to be a unique individual. It is strong when each feels that he or she is a distinct, valuable individual as well as part of a valuable relationship.

One of the fundamentals of a long-lasting love is giving ourselves the right to fulfill our own potential as well as encouraging our lover to do the same. Although giving this freedom to oneself and, especially, to a lover may take learning, the pay-off is great—a strong, healthy, rewarding marriage that never stops growing.

The same is true for sex. Great sex comes from both partners knowing that their individual uniqueness is respected and cherished. Each lover finds satisfaction while giving their partner the opportunity to find satisfaction. Differences in desires and needs are lovingly encouraged, harmonized and fulfilled.

Great sex is the ultimate in sharing. Stated simply, great sex occurs when two lovers both realize their emotional and physical desires. Great sex may call for some sexual skills, but more than skills it requires generous sharing. Like ice skaters in the couples competition of the Olympics, lovers desiring great sex need to perform simultaneously as a team and as individuals.

Great sex begins with each of us being willing

and able to satisfy our individual desires. People who are confident that they can fulfill their personal needs (whether on their own or with help) make good team players. Being confident about having your own desires satisfied allows you to pay greater attention to the cares and desires of your lover. Love, warmth, caring, tenderness and interest in your lover all grow with self-confidence.

Satisfying your own sexual desires requires you to be both sexually knowledgeable and willing to ask for help from your lover. From the first kiss to the last, each of you must seek the kind of caring, sensual pleasure and sexual pleasure you want. If one of you desires more or different sexual activity from the other, you have to be willing to ask for it. This doesn't mean ignoring what your lover wants. It just means making sure that your own desires are fulfilled so that you feel good about whatever you're doing. Far from ignoring your lover's wishes, you'll most likely pay more attention to your lover as you find that one of the most rewarding aspects of sex is giving physical pleasure to one's lover.

The goal is learning to turn this individual search for sexual fulfillment into mutual fulfillment. Although each partner is seeking personal satisfaction, each needs to proceed in a manner that results in satisfaction for both. The result is a sharing of love and pleasure that is seldom achieved any other way. Even after love-making is over, both lovers have a lasting memory of reality and fantasy united in one glorious experience.

Staying realistic about marriage and sex is equally

important. Too often, lovers believe that they exist completely as a couple and develop unrealistic expectations of each other. Each of us needs to remember that we only have control over ourselves. Some couples often become unrealistically concerned about simultaneous orgasm, or any orgasm, forgetting to enjoy all the other sexual pleasures. Unfortunately, both sexes too often feel compelled to create the illusion of "success" by faking orgasm.

Now is the time for the two of you to to fine-tune your intercourse skills. It's well worth the time and effort.

Forget about how you used to participate in sex and instead begin to think about how you want to participate. As you know by now, the two of you may have considerably different sexual desires. No matter what each of you wants sex to be, you both deserve to enjoy sex your own way; the challenge is to learn how to not only allow, but actually enhance sex in the way you both want it—both physically and emotionally.

You need to begin by being sure you can understand and can acknowledge the major variations in physical functioning between the sexes. The most obvious difference is the ease of getting excited and reaching orgasm. Men usually get excited more easily and sooner than women. Too often the husband reaches orgasm before his wife, and sex ends before both are totally satisfied. This can be even more complicated because most men easily become extremely excited through intercourse, while some women have difficulty getting excited and reaching orgasm at all through intercourse. Often both lovers are left disappointed.

The solution to getting each partner sexually excited at the same time is relatively easy. Just use the skills that you have developed throughout this course to control your own sexual arousal. For men, this often means slowing down; for women, it generally means keeping arousal growing. This is the time for the man to pace himself while he assists his wife. This is the time for the wife to use the skill she's learned for contracting her pelvic-floor muscles described on pages 85 to 87. The effects will help arouse her and can be exciting for both. For women who still have trouble becoming aroused through intercourse, more manual stimulation (before and during penetration) and varying the intercourse position may provide the answer.

Your assignment now is to put the finishing touches on the sex life you want. You'll learn to accept and enjoy your individual differences in desire and in physical functioning. Specifically, you'll learn to enjoy five minutes of sexual intercourse. Learning to enjoy intercourse for this long will give you immense control over your own sex life as well as the freedom to thoroughly enjoy the pleasures of great sex. Five minutes may seem to some of you like a long time, but it's not just possible, it's reasonable. As always, the key to success is simply enjoying the pleasure of the moment while eliminating any discomfort.

Once again, schedule three practice sessions. Before your first session, get a watch with a second hand to help you monitor your progress. Also, make sure that both of you feel comfortable with your method of birth control or lack of it. If you are using a method that is acceptable to both of you, or if you have agreed not to use birth control, fine. But if either of you is uncomfortable about the method or lack of one, face this issue now. Discuss the subject openly. Discuss your fears and concerns with each other. If you have questions that need explanation, contact a physician or family-planning clinic. If you do not get rid of this discomfort, you will always find it standing in your way.

Remember that this is *your* session, so make it special for yourself. When you begin, take your time and allow yourself to enjoy all of the previous steps. Kiss, hug, talk, pet or do whatever you both want. Whatever feels good. Take pleasure in it as a couple. Don't go faster than is comfortable.

This is also your lover's session. Like you, your lover needs to make the session special. Give your lover freedom and encouragement. Listen to your lover's desires and help whenever you can. As you each make the session special for yourself, make it special for your lover.

When you both feel comfortable, get into a position for intercourse. This doesn't mean that you need to do it abruptly. It should gradually follow what you've been doing. For these sessions limit your intercourse positions to either the missionary position (man on top) or the reverse (woman on top). Gradually put the penis into the vagina, but first make sure that each of you is ready. The man should have a stiff enough erection so that his penis enters easily. The woman should have relatively loose vaginal muscles and enough vaginal lubrication so that the entering penis doesn't cause her pain. If her muscles are loose but vaginal lubrication is not sufficient, you can use a lubricant such as K-Y jelly or vaseline.

Try to keep up the intercourse for five minutes. Stroke as much as you can and rest whenever necessary. Continue to kiss, hug, hold or do whatever else you both enjoy. Simply make it enjoyable for both of you as you practice extending the length of time of intercourse. The husband should try to delay orgasm until the end of the five minutes. The wife should feel free to have orgasm whenever and however often she wants. If either of you wants more stimulation during the five minutes, try manual stimulation of the genitals. If you want less stimulation, slow down or stop the thrusting, or maybe even off and on think about something other than sex.

If either of you feels uncomfortable, signal, stop whatever you're doing and suggest a solution. If necessary, rest for a few minutes. When you're comfortable, try again. For these sessions, it is important to extend your definitions of discomfort to include the potential discomforts of intercourse. The husband needs to include in his definition a too-soft penis, which is not unusual and just a sign that he is not yet ready. Men also need to include in their definition the uncontrollable urge to have orgasm before they want to. In contrast, women need to be concerned about pain and lack of lubrication. It is not unusual for the wife to feel pain when the penis enters. Pain is usually caused by lack of lubrication and generally means that the female is not yet excited enough. Just remember that the man should not attempt intercourse before having a strong erection and the woman should not seek it before being well lubricated. Pain for the woman may also be caused by the penis forcing itself through the opening of her vagina or by the penis hitting the top of her vagina. These situations usually result when the woman is not sufficiently relaxed for the vagina to open wide enough or extend far enough. Waiting until the woman reaches a high enough level of excitement is usually the answer. Altering the position may also help. However, if there seems to be no reasonable explanation for pain, the wife should probably see a doctor.

Finally, remember to enjoy the peaceful time at the end of each intercourse session. Take advantage of the feelings of closeness and bliss combined with the pleasant memories. But, keep in mind that men and women often enjoy this time in very different ways: the man often likes to sleep and the woman often likes to share physical closeness with her lover. Simply ask for what you want and then find a way that allows each of you to feel fulfilled.

Schedule your three intercourse classes now. If you both succeed in giving your partner and yourself the individual pleasure you've wanted for five minutes of intercourse and each enjoy orgasm during two consecutive sessions, great. You will have not only finished the final session, you will have finished the course. This calls for a celebration—but the real rewards are those that will continue to come to you in the future.

If you want to practice more, feel free to schedule as many additional practice sessions as you would like. However, if at any time after the three sessions, you find that you aren't progressing as quickly as you would like, read Alternative 1. Also, keep up the rewards—physical, verbal and tangible—all of them.

Here's the list of possible types of discomfort. Signal discomfort if either of you feel:

- Anxious, nervous, afraid, up tight, edgy, or angry;
- Too hot, too cold or aware of any other specific physical discomfort;
- Guilty, ashamed or disgusted;
- Rushed or pressured;
- Compelled to attempt something not prescribed by the program or not wanting to attempt something that had been prescribed;
- Your body responding unpleasantly or not at all. (For example, did you have tight muscles, pain, loss of erection, premature or delayed orgasm, or lack of lubrication?)

ALTERNATIVE 1

Some aspect of intercourse is apparently causing you discomfort. A good way to get this under control is by using the imagination sessions that we have been describing as alternatives throughout this course. If you have tried them, you already know that if you can become comfortable imagining an activity, you can learn to enjoy it in reality. And that the more pleasurable it is in your imagination, the more pleasurable it will be when it actually happens.

Take a break from your joint practice sessions. Instead, for the partner who is feeling discomfort, schedule four individual ten-minute sessions for the next few days. During these sessions, practice using your imagination to create and eliminate discomfort.

Find a comfortable chair where you can lean back, put your feet up and relax. Close your eyes, take a few deep breaths and feel your body slowing down. When you feel relatively peaceful, imagine whatever is for you a very pleasant scene: lying on a beach after swimming, sitting on your deck in the sun or doing something you enjoy very much. Try to picture this scene as completely as possible and enjoy the feelings associated with it. Stretch your imagination so that it's almost as good as being there.

When you are able to vividly imagine yourself in this pleasant scene for a minute, end it and imagine yourself having intercourse with your lover. Try to feel all of the emotions. Enjoy the pleasure and acknowledge the discomfort. Actually try to experience the discomfort that arises in the practice situation. As soon as you begin to feel it, end the practice scene and bring back the pleasurable scene until the discomfort goes away.

Repeat this process for the duration of the ten-minute session. Each time you imagine yourself involved in intercourse, try to feel a little more pleasure than the previous time. Eventually, even picture yourself reaching orgasm through intercourse. Try to see and feel all the excitement and ecstasy. Little by little you will find yourself working through the discomfort and creating the pleasure you're seeking.

After at least four imagery sessions, schedule three intercourse sessions. If you become uncomfortable during a session, signal your partner and suggest a solution. To help reduce your discomfort, recall the pleasant scene in your imagination. As soon as you're comfortable again, continue the session. Whenever discomfort returns, create the pleasant imagery.

If you are successful in eliminating discomfort during the five minutes of intercourse and in having satisfying orgasm during the practice sessions, you have completed the course and it's time to celebrate. If you are still encountering difficulties, read the following alternative.

ALTERNATIVE 2

You are apparently having some difficulty enjoying five minutes of intercourse and orgasm. Whether your difficulties are with the act of intercourse itself or with reaching five minutes, the solution is the same.

If you are having difficulties with initial penetration, begin by having either one of you hold the penis next to, but not inside the vagina. When you are able to do this comfortably for fifteen seconds, you are ready to move on to the next step. Now put the head of the penis into the vagina, but without any movement. When you are able to do this comfortably for fifteen seconds, put the entire penis into the vagina, but again without any movement. When you have done this, you have mastered the basic step of entry.

When you are comfortable with the act of penetration, it is important for each of you to become comfortable with the penis in the vagina for a prolonged period. Your new goal is to remain comfortable for five minutes of penetration with little or no genital movement. Since you are able to remain comfortable for fiteen seconds, set a goal of thirty seconds, then one minute, two minutes, three minutes, four minutes, and eventually five minutes. If you encounter difficulty reaching any of your goals, simply set another shorter goal first. When you reach five minutes of comfort without movement, you are halfway through the session.

Your next step is to remain comfortable for five minutes of intercourse *with* regular movement. Start with fifteen seconds of thrusting and then remain still for the remainder of the five minutes. When you are successful for fifteen seconds, extend the movement to thirty seconds. Gradually increase the time to five minutes of intercourse, including three minutes of movement. The movement need not be continuous. You may want to do some thrusting, rest a little, and then thrust some more; maybe alternate one minute of movement followed by one minute of rest.

When you are comfortable with three minutes of movement during the five minutes of intercourse, it's time to put away the clock. Simply enjoy the intercourse and all the emotions that go with it. Let yourself get lost in the pleasure of the moment.

Throughout, make sure you acknowledge and eliminate discomfort as soon as it arises. Use any techniques, including imagery, to help you. Diverting your attention away from your performance should help you easily and quickly increase the length of time of intercourse. Imagining the pleasant scene of the imagery session may help. Once you have extended the time, cut back on the use of the pleasant imagery. If you still feel pain or discomfort, you may want to try a different position or remove the penis from the vagina and return to manual stimulation before resuming intercourse. If the vagina is still not lubricated enough or the penis is not hard enough for easy entry, return to manual stimulation before entry. If the penis becomes soft, remove it from the vagina and return to enjoying other types of sexual stimulation.

Don't get discouraged if progress is slow at times. It's likely that after maintaining the same level of success for some time, you will be able to make some big jumps. No matter what, it's very important that you keep trying. Success will come with practice.

When you both are able to enjoy five minutes of intercourse, you have completed this alternative. If you both are also able to reach orgasm, you are now sex-education graduates. If you are still having some difficulty, read Alternative 3.

ALTERNATIVE 3

Now that you have mastered the "technical skills" of intercourse, your goal for this alternative is to increase stimulation. You need to learn to let your mind go, while increasing the physical stimulation of your genitals.

Freeing your mind should not be difficult. Since you are already reaching orgasm manually, you most likely have freed your imagination quite a bit. Remember that sex should be fun and that it is not a win-or-lose contest. Try to find what it takes to put a little more zest into your sex life.

During intercourse try varying your positions. Sometimes, individuals get more stimulation in one position than another. Both partners may find added stimulation if the female contracts her pelvic-floor muscles (see the exercise on pages 85 to 87). Experiment until you find the positions that work best for both of you.

Finally, add more manual stimulation. Sometimes, thrusting during intercourse just isn't enough stimulation to bring some people to orgasm. Going back to the basics and increasing stimulation manually is sometimes necessary. This is more often true for women than for men. Spend some extra time, before and during intercourse, on manual stimulation, especially during intercourse. It is often exceptionally arousing to manually stroke one's lover's genitals during thrusting. In addition, feel free to take breaks from thrusting to manually stroke your lover's or your own genitals. If you enjoy oral sex, now is a great time. Whatever you try, simply attempt to get yourselves close to orgasm through manual stimulation so that intercourse will extend this excitement to the point of orgasm.

Basically, the instructions for this alternative are for you to experiment to find what works best for the two of you. Try as much variety as you can. Discover what you enjoy best and acknowledge discomfort whenever it arises.

Keep practicing until you both are able to reach satisfying orgasm through intercourse. Consider yourselves graduates of the course when you can reach orgasm through the combination of intercourse and manual stimulation. Since you both are able to reach orgasm through manual stimulation, this should not be too difficult. A little experimentation and common sense should lead to rewarding results.

CHAPTER 14

Things to Remember

1. Marriage deserves thought and effort.

A lasting love deserves the lifelong care and thought we would use to preserve and protect anything precious. Couples should put the same energy into keeping their marriage alive and vital that they would expect to put into their careers and children.

2. Sex is a big part of every marriage.

Whether a couple talks about it or ignores it, their sex life greatly influences how they feel about themselves, each other and their marriage. A gratifying sex life not only makes marriage better, but makes all of life a little better. Satisfying sex leads to a greater appreciation of sex itself, one's partner and oneself. While a satisfying sexual relationship can't necessarily save a marriage, the absence of a satisfying sex life can certainly impair one.

3. The key to a rich sex life is sexual comfort.

The best sex occurs when the partners have each learned to be comfortable with their own and their lover's sexuality. As this happens, each becomes more and more satisfied with the sexual relationship. Feelings grow deeper and desires occur more frequently.

4. Sex is more than orgasm.

Sex often begins with a touch, a smile or a friendly word. It includes hugs, kisses, petting and intercourse. It's love, passion and great physical pleasure. And it's also fantasies, fun, dreams and memories. Really enjoying love-making means enjoying every stage of sex from the first spark to orgasm to the heavenly feelings afterwards.

5. You and your partner are each great sex partners.

You were each born with the ability to enjoy sex, but for whatever reason, your desires, feelings and performance may have been limited. Satisfying sex comes from learning to let your sexual feelings and behavior surface naturally. Simply accepting each other without reservation leads to a much closer marriage, and your acceptance allows each of you to risk more and to give more.

6. Lasting passion comes from a combination of friendship, trust and romance.

Passion is a powerful emotion, and giving in to it means openly showing feelings and taking risks. We take such risk only with people we trust. This trust comes from the feeling of acceptance that we get from friendship. Romance adds the feeling that we're special. This combination of friendship, trust and romance keeps a marriage alive and growing.

7. Happiness in marriage and sex begins with accepting responsiblity for oneself.

You and your spouse are a couple, but you are also two individuals who are each trying to be comfortable with life. You each need to take care of your own needs, while allowing your partner to take care of his or hers. You need to accept yourself as you are and let yourself be who you want to be. You need to give yourself what you want, both physically and emotionally. When you want your partner's help, you need to ask for it. If you don't ask, you can't expect to receive. However, even if you do ask, it doesn't mean that you will always get the help that you ask for. As you and your spouse each learn to take better care of yourselves, the two of you will find yourselves more caring of each other.

8. The special ingredient that makes life—and sex—special is play.

Much of a marriage is not aimed at accomplishing anything in particular except simply enjoying each other's company. This is particularly true with sex—it is simply a way for two people to share their love, emotional pleasure, and physical pleasure, and have fun together.

9. Great sex and a great marriage are the ultimate in sharing.

Great sex occurs when two lovers both realize their emotional and physical desires. Great sex may call for some sexual skills, but more than skills it requires generous sharing. Great sex comes from both partners knowing that their individual uniqueness is respected and cherished. Each lover finds satisfaction while giving his or her partner the opportunity to find satisfaction. Differences in desires and needs are lovingly encouraged, harmonized and fulfilled. Your goal is learning to turn this individual search for fulfillment into mutual fulfillment.

Other New Harbinger Self-Help Titles

The Marriage Bed: Renewing Love, Friendship, Trust, and Romance, $11.95
Focal Group Psychotherapy, $44.95
Hot Water Therapy: How to Save Your Back, Neck & Shoulders in Ten Minutes a Day of Exercise, $11.95
Older & Wiser: A Workbook for Coping With Aging, $12.95
Prisoners of Belief: Exposing & Changing Beliefs that Control Your Life, $10.95
Be Sick Well: A Healthy Approach to Chronic Illness, $11.95
Men & Grief: A Guide for Men Surviving the Death of a Loved One, $11.95
When the Bough Breaks: A Helping Guide for Parents of Sexually Abused Children, $11.95
Love Addiction: A Guide to Emotional Independence, $11.95
When Once Is Not Enough: Help for Obsessive Compulsives, $11.95
The New Three Minute Meditator, $9.95
Getting to Sleep, $10.95
The Relaxation & Stress Reduction Workbook, 3rd Edition, $13.95
Leader's Guide to the Relaxation & Stress Reduction Workbook, $19.95
Beyond Grief: A Guide for Recovering from the Death of a Loved One, $10.95
Thoughts & Feelings: The Art of Cognitive Stress Intervention, $13.95
Messages: The Communication Skills Book, $12.95
The Divorce Book, $11.95
Hypnosis for Change: A Manual of Proven Techniques, 2nd Edition, $12.95
The Deadly Diet: Recovering from Anorexia & Bulimia, $11.95
Self-Esteem, $12.95
Acquiring Courage: An Audio Cassette for the Rapid Treatment of Phobias, $14.95
The Better Way to Drink, $11.95
Chronic Pain Control Workbook, $13.95
Rekindling Desire: Bringing Your Sexual Relationship Back to Life, $12.95
Life Without Fear: Anxiety and Its Cure, $10.95
Visualization for Change, $12.95
Guideposts to Meaning: Discovering What Really Matters, $11.95
Controlling Stagefright, $11.95
Videotape: Clinical Hypnosis for Stress & Anxiety Reduction, $24.95
Starting Out Right: Essential Parenting Skills for Your Child's First Years, $12.95
Big Kids: A Parent's Guide to Weight Control for Children, $11.95
Personal Peace: Transcending Your Interpersonal Limits, $11.95
My Parent's Keeper: Adult Children of the Emotionally Disturbed, $11.95
When Anger Hurts, $12.95
Free of the Shadows: Recovering from Sexual Violence, $12.95
Resolving Conflict With Others and Within Yourself, $12.95
Lifetime Weight Control, $11.95
The Anxiety & Phobia Workbook, $13.95
Love and Renewal: A Couple's Guide to Commitment, $12.95
The Habit Control Workbook, $12.95

Send a check for the titles you want, plus $2.00 for shipping and handling, to:

New Harbinger Publications, Inc.
5674 Shattuck Avenue
Oakland, CA 94609

Or write for a free catalog of all our quality self-help publications. For orders over $20 call 1-800-748-6273. Have your Visa or Mastercard number ready.